THE
BIGGEST E[...]

TIM VINE
JOKE BOOK

Tim Vine is a comedian. He was born in Cheam. He's a big fan of broccoli and darts and karaoke.

THIS TIM VINE JOKE BOOK BELONGS TO

....

MY FAVOURITE JOKE IS JOKE NUMBER

....

THE BIGGEST EVER TIM VINE JOKE BOOK

C

CENTURY · LONDON

Published by Century 2010

29

Copyright © Tim Vine 2010

First published in Great Britain in 2010 by
Century
Random House, 20 Vauxhall Bridge Road,
London SW1V 2SA

www.randomhouse.co.uk

Illustrations © Tim Vine 2010

Addresses for companies within The Random House Group Limited can be found at:
www.randomhouse.co.uk

The Random House Group Limited Reg. No. 954009

A CIP catalogue record for this book
is available from the British Library

ISBN 978 1 8460 5827 1

Penguin Random House is committed to a sustainable future for
our business, our readers and our planet. This book is made from
Forest Stewardship Council® certified paper.

Printed and bound in Great Britain by Clays Ltd, Elcograf S.p.A.

Typeset in Bailey Sans by Palimpsest Book Production Limited,
Falkirk, Stirlingshire

For my family, my friends and all of my fan

PREFACE

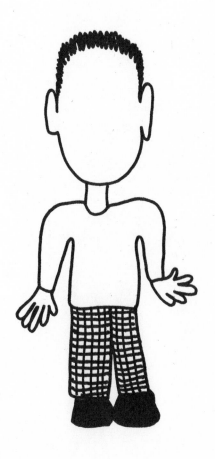

INTRODUCTION

So this bloke rang me up. He said, 'I'm calling from Random House.' I said, 'Can you be a bit more specific?' (That's the first joke.) He said, 'Would you like to create a joke book filled entirely with your gags?' I said, 'As long as I don't have to put the cover on myself, cos that would be a bit of a bind.' (That's the second joke but I might be losing you.) He said, 'What do you know about books?' I said, 'Only what I've read.' (It's the way he types 'em!) He said, 'Fill the book with nonsense.' I said, 'That's my middle name . . . Phil.'

The result of that first exchange is in your hands. Jokes I wrote for my stand up act, jokes from some of my old Edinburgh shows and tours, jokes I wrote in little note-books that I stashed in the cupboard under the stairs and thought would never see the light of day, jokes I wrote with my mate John Archer – just lots of my jokes. And I've also scribbled some in cartoon form.

I hope you laugh. The advantage of a book, of course, is that I won't hear the heckles.

Tim Vine
2010

TIM VINE JOKES: 1 TO 100

1. This bloke said to me, he said I once got my dog to retrieve a stick from 100 miles away. I said that's a bit far-fetched.

2. I don't like my hands. I always keep them at arm's length.

3. This reporter said to me, he said how would you describe the absence of Haley's flaming meteorite? I said no comet.

4. I'm amazed how many people go to Ascot when it's windy. Still, hats off to them.

5. Me and my brother inherited some furniture from the local zoo. I'm glad to say I got the lion's chair.

6. Whenever I'm in Italy I become a rickety old table. I guess I'm just a hopeless Rome antique.

7. My granddad was a film actor a very long time ago. He was a star of the bronze screen.

8. Dot dot dot. Dash dash dash. I really regret that. Remorse code.

9. After I've had an argument I sometimes hold a Hoover over my head.
It helps clear the air.

10. The other day I sat on a hairdryer.
That put the wind up me.

11. So I was lying in a bath of meths, and my girlfriend rang up and said she was lying in a bath of paraffin.
I said I'm with you in spirit.

12. I've got a friend who's a very tall blade of grass. He's easily swayed.

13. This bloke said to me, he said I bet you can't name a famous Egyptian landmark.
I said that's what you Sphinx.

14. My dog's bark is worse than his bite because he hasn't got any teeth, and when he barks people's ears explode.

15. I saw a 20-foot parrot the other day. You could knock me down with a feather.

16. I was adopted by a sports car. He took me under his wing mirror.

17. I was skiing through Tie Rack and I fell down an 80-foot cravat.

18. So I saw this bloke who was a cross between an ostrich and a serial killer. He was always burying other people's heads in the sand.

19. The other day I tied my head to a dog's tail. I just fancied a bit of a chinwag.

20. So I saw this bloke with a 1.2-litre engine halfway down his arm.
I said more power to your elbow.

21. Conjunctivitis.com – that's a site for sore eyes.

22. I was watching a horror film and my skin peeled off my body and started tiptoeing round the house. I thought, this film is making my skin creep.

23. I've got a friend who's a psychopath and he's got a brilliant sense of humour. He kills me!

24. So this bloke pulled a vital organ out of my chest and chucked it into a pond. My heart sank.

25. This bloke said to me, he said why are you shouting into the air conditioning? I said I'm venting my feelings.

HELL FOR LEATHER.

26. I saw this extinct bird with a hunchback. It was Quasidodo.

27. I've started displaying some of my clothes and possessions and photographs of me. I've made an exhibition of myself.

28. I didn't have a happy upbringing. I remember my 3rd birthday party. I was 15.

29. The Second World War was no picnic. (Because they couldn't find a big enough blanket).

30. So I went to the petrol station. I said, fill her up. When I came back he was stuffing my wife's face with cream cakes.

31. This turkey challenged me to a fight. He threw down the giblet.

32. I saw this angry verruca. He was on the wart path.

33. So I went on a date and all we talked about was wooden leg extensions. The conversation was stilted.

34. I'm looking for a house at the moment. It's MY house. I've forgotten where I live.

35. I spent the whole of today pruning. I was just chucking prunes at people.

LIGHTNING
REACTIONS

36. My girlfriend is covered from head to toe in grass. Her name's Lorna.

37. Me and my mum don't get on. We never argue, but if a bus stops in front of us we don't get on.

38. My uncle's mad because he wears a wiggly jacket. Whereas my auntie, she wears a straight jacket.

39. I entered a competition putting sails on boats. It was rigged.

40. So I went down the local hotel, and I said can you put me up, and he nailed me to the ceiling.

41. I've got a friend who puts plaster of
    Paris on my face, waits for it to dry
    and then hits it with a chisel.
    He cracks me up.

42. Groundsheets. They don't get much
    coverage.

43. I've got a gun made out of a dozen pigs.
    It's a 12-boar.

44. This bloke said to me, he said why
    have you got manure on your head?
    I said I've just had my hair dung.

45. What has lots of legs and a machine
    gun?
    A caterkiller.

SKI-JUMPER

46. I saw a coconut-flavoured biscuit playing football. It was Wayne Macarooney.

47. So I went to the chemists, I said give me some rat poison. He said, I'm sorry sir, but we only sell things to unblock your nose. I said, I know that, but I've got a rat up my nose.

48. This bloke said to me, he said I live in the sky with a Swiss clock. I said you're in cloud cuckoo land.

49. I once tried to hang myself with a clip-on tie. Broke both my legs.

50. I used to file my nails but then I thought, what's the point of keeping them?

51. Exit signs, they're on the way out.

52. Black Beauty, he's a dark horse.

53. I've got a sponge front door.
Hey, don't knock it.

54. I never sleep with fish.
I'm halibut.

55. I used to go out with a mackerel and
when we split up she was very upset.
I said, there's plenty more men on the
earth.

56. I'm being stalked by a Sumo wrestler.
I've got a big following.

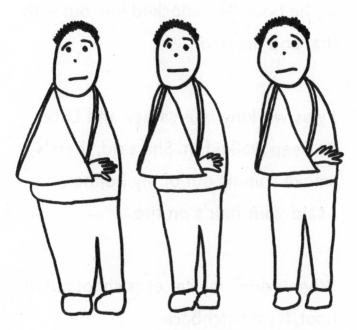

DISLOCATION
DISLOCATION
DISLOCATION

57. I was driving here and a policeman stopped me because one of my tyres was a bit flat. Luckily I had a foot pump in the boot. So I knocked him out with that and drove off.

58. I was working in a garage and Little Bo Peep walked in. She said, there's smoke coming out of my bonnet.
I said your hair's on fire.

59. When I drive my car eggs shoot out the boot. It's a hatchback.

60. I'm colour blind but it doesn't stop me enjoying life. The other night I saw 'Joseph and His Amazing Brown Coat'.
It was great.

61. I was working in a health food shop and this bloke walked in. He said, evening primrose oil? I said Mr Vine to you.

62. He said, soya chunks? I said, you shouldn't have been looking.

63. He said, cellulite? I said, how much do you want for it?

64. He said, would you like some Alpen? I said, I suppose you think that's a muesli.

65. So I got a job at Burger King and Andrew Lloyd Webber walked in. He said, give me 2 Whoppers. I said, you're good looking and your musicals are great.

66. Batman walked up to me, smashed a vase over my head and said, T'pow! I said, don't you mean Kapow? He said, no, I've got china in my hand.

67. You invented Tippex – Correct me if I'm wrong.

68. So I was in this restaurant and during the starter the waiter came over, tapped me on the head with his little finger and then walked off. Then during the main course he got his index finger and applied gentle pressure to my shoulder. And then while I was having dessert he brushed my ear lightly with his thumb. That's the difference between a good restaurant and a great restaurant. It's the little touches.

69. So I said to the waiter, I said give me something herby. So he gave me a Volkswagen Beetle with no driver.

70. So I was in the jungle and I saw this monkey with a tin-opener. I said, you don't need a tin-opener to peel a banana. He said, I know, this is for the custard.

71. This rabbit walked up to me. He said, someone's just chopped off one of my feet. I said that's lucky, isn't it.

72. He said, I'm a male rabbit and I'm not moving. I said, oh I see. The buck stops here.

73. He said, are you lookin' at me?
It was Rabbit DeNiro.

74. So I looked round and there was a partridge, a grouse and a pheasant, all dressed as clowns – Game for a laugh.

75. I'll tell you what makes my blood boil – Crematoriums.

76. I've always been very lazy. I've got a smoke alarm that's got a snooze button.

77. I was going to write my will today but then I thought, life's too short.

78. I saw one of those motorbikes with the roof that goes right over the top. I couldn't believe it. I thought someone had hot-wired a photo booth.

79. I was working in a travel agents and this bloke walked in. He said, I want to book a flight, very short notice. I said you've just missed it.

80. He said, I want to go somewhere hot and secluded. So I locked him in the photocopy room.

81. Today I went shoplifting while balanced on the shoulders of a group of vampires. I was done for theft on 4 counts.

82. People with guns who say give me your money. You've got to hand it to them.

83. I was a terrible builder. When the foreman said to me, have you got a plumb line? I said, the one I usually use is 'have you got a plum?'

THOUGHTFUL SEAGULL

84. So I went to my GP and said, I feel like I've been hit on the head by a set of bongos. He said, you've probably got slight percussion.

85. He said, you're turning into an airport. I said is it terminal?

86. He said, antiseptic? I said, I've got nothing against the Jews.

87. Do you ever get that, when you're halfway through eating a horse and you think to yourself, I'm not as hungry as I thought I was.

88. I've got a horse called Treacle. He's got golden stirrups.

PASTA SAYINGS

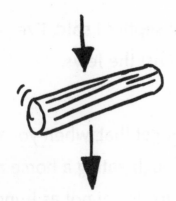

The Penne drops.

89. He doesn't go out much, he's a shire horse.

90. That's 3 horse jokes on the trot. Four!

91. So I went to the hair salon and my Dad's sister came in spinning round in circles. I thought, oh my giddy aunt.

92. So I said to this bloke, I said I'm going to Buckingham Palace to do Prince Philip's hair. He said, have you got a permit? I said, no, I've just got to take a bit off the back.

93. I said, do you like my shirt? It's covered in pictures of cactuses. He said, cacti? I said, never mind the tie, what do you think of the shirt?

94. So I was playing the piano in a bar and an elephant walked in. As I was playing he started crying his eyes out. I said, do you recognise the tune? He said, no, I recognise the ivory.

95. I went to the head office of the RSPCA today. It's absolutely tiny. You couldn't swing a cat in there.

96. Today I had dinner with my boss and his wife and it was a complete disaster. My boss's wife said to me, how many potatoes would you like? I said, I'll just have one. She said, it's alright you don't have to be polite. I said, alright then, I'll just have one you stupid cow.

PARACHUTING MISTAKES

Canoe

97. So I went down the local department store. I said, have you got any net curtains? He said, no, they've all got VAT on them. I said that's gross.

98. I said, I can't decide whether to buy this bed or not. He said, do you want to sleep on it? I said of course I do.

99. I said, how much is it? He said, 98.99. I said make your mind up.

100. I'm against the arms race. It's bad for your elbows.

101. This bloke said to me, he said do you have any strong political views? I said, no I don't, you capitalist Europhobe.

102. I rang up pest control. I said vermin? He said no he just left.

103. I threw a stick in the sea and a round floating object brought it back to me. I said there's a good buoy.

104. Then a bag of cement went past at 100 miles an hour. I thought, that's quicksand.

105. Did you know the word 'receding' is 400 years old? And that's going back a bit.

AN IMPARTIAL ECLIPSE

106. I used to work for King Midas but he gave me the golden handshake.

107. So I went to the doctors, I said, I've got Irish voices coming out of my tummy. He said you've got a stomach Ulster.

108. I said, why have I got crow's feet on the side of my eyes? He said there's a crow sitting on your forehead.

109. My ankle keeps falling off and it doesn't cost anything to find me attractive – Footloose and fancy-free.

110. I spent the last two weeks sitting on a large hard book. It was my annual holiday.

A NET PROPHET

111. So I went to the pants shop, I said my name is Fronts and I want to put some pants on my head. He said Y-fronts? I said none of your business.

112. I said I want to see some underwear. He said it's under there. I said under where? He said I heard you the first time.

113. My mum's into role reversal. She puts the ham on the outside.

114. Someone said to me that lemons were very sharp so I tried using one to carve a turkey.

115. So I said to this policeman, I said you look like a tube of Evostik. He arrested me for solvent abuse.

THE PROFESSOR SUDDENLY
REALISED THE KNEE ON HIS
RIGHT LEG HAD REVERSED
ITSELF.

116. So I went to the opticians. He said, how many fingers am I holding up? I said 17,251. He said wrong. Three. But I tell you what, you can't half count quick.

117. I did some cross-dressing this morning. I said where are my flipping socks!

118. I saw these two citrus fruits having a fight. It was satsuma wrestling.

119. This woman said to me, she said I've got designs on you. Then she showed me a diagram of my spleen.

120. I used to be a teddy boy. I had two furry ears either side of my head.

121. The other day someone burnt
     the bottom of my shoes. It was
     soul-destroying.

122. My Christmas decorations are inflatable.
     I'm forever blowing baubles.

123. I refuse to work in a coal mine.
     It's beneath me.

124. I met a fox who was brilliant at football.
     It was Brazil Brush.

125. I've just been on a crash diet. I drove
     my car into a tree and spent a month
     on a drip.

DRAWING ANY BIRD IN THE
DISTANCE IS EASY.

126. This bloke said to me, he said I'm going to sell two flats. I thought, ooh, premises premises.

127. I thought Tom Cruise was a boating holiday for male cats.

128. Actually my name isn't Tim Vine, it's Tim Buktoo. Sorry, I was miles away.

129. I went to a posh party and everyone was drinking and knitting. I got Pimms and needles.

130. I'm on a seabed diet. If I see a bed I eat it.

131. Frozen apples. They're hardcore.

132. Whenever I wash up I get covered in soapy bubbles. It's Sud's Law.

133. My local village was destroyed by toilet paper. Everyone was wiped out.

134. So I was in the party shop with my granny. She said, this kaleidoscope's rubbish. I said that's a balloon-pump.

135. So I saw this dolphin serial killer. It was Jack the Flipper.

136. So I was on this train, I said, I don't think much of this bunk bed.
He said that's the luggage rack.

137. This bloke said to me, he said do you ever talk off the top of your head?
I said no. Halfway down at the front.

138. I went on holiday with my horse.
It was self-cantering.

139. So I said to this bloke, I said when I was on holiday I stayed in a bed and breakfast. He said half-board? I said no, I was totally bored.

140. I was a rubbish church window cleaner.
I got rid of all the stains.

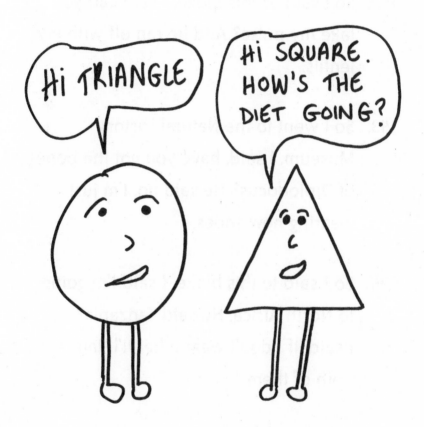

141. This bloke said to me, he said shall we talk about diaries? I said Letts.

142. So I said to this bloke, I said can you take my pulse? And he ran off with my lentils.

143. So I went to the Natural History Museum. I said, have you got the bones of Diplodocus? He said no, I'm just wearing new shoes.

144. So I said to this bloke, I said I'm going to North Africa. He said Tanzania? I said, if I don't wear a hat it'll tan both of them.

145. This bloke said to me, he said you look like a medieval string instrument. I said are you calling me a lyre?

DOUBLE CHIN.

146. In 2002 the Queen had been on
     the throne for 50 years.
     Would JUBILEE vit?

147. This bloke said to me, he said are you a
     high flyer? I said no, I tend to hand out
     flyers at waist level.

148. I went to the haberdashery. I was
     looking for a cheap frill.

149. I went down the local opticians. I
     said have you got a contact lens
     solution? He said what about laser
     surgery?

150. This bloke said to me, he said I'm the
     brother of River Phoenix. I said you
     must be Joaquin.

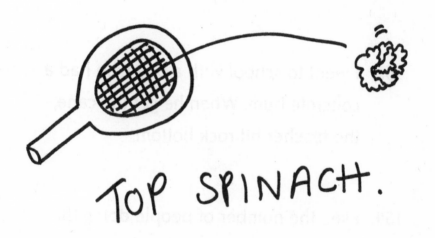

TOP SPINACH.

151. I fell in love with a clumsy cleaner. She swept me off my feet.

152. Have you seen that great cricketing cook? Chef Boycott.

153. I went to school with a boy who had a concrete bum. When he got the cane, the teacher hit rock bottom.

154. I see the number of people doing the high jump has leapt up.

155. So I said to a friend of mine, I said how come your sofa is covered in burnt patches? He said my dog's been molten.

LARK DE TRIUMPHE

156. Did you know 30% of car accidents
in Sweden involve a moose?
I say don't let them drive.

157. Wyoming. Sounds like Flash Gordon
begging for mercy.

158. Apparently 1 in 13 Americans
have worked for Macdonalds.
The other 12 got rejected.

159. The other day I couldn't decide
whether to buy a packet of guitar
strings or a box of eggs. It was six of
one and half a dozen of the other.

160. I can see through your smile.
(Because you've got glass teeth.)

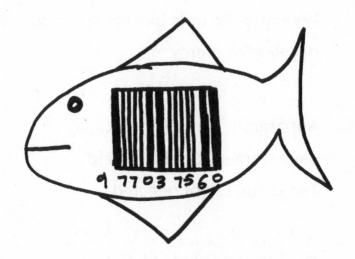

BAR COD

161. When I was offered a place at the College of Leapfrog I jumped at the chance.

162. The guitarist of U2 is called The Edge. When he was at school he was a border.

163. What's the secret of comedy about tea? Twining.

164. I went down to my local town hall. I said, this town is in a mess, what are you going to do about it? He said, nothing. I said why not? He said this is an aerobics class.

165. Curries. Wouldn't touch them with a bhaji pole.

166. I just got a text from Heaven.
That was a Godsend.

167. I came here on a sheet of sandpaper.
It was a bit of a rough ride.

168. This bloke said to me, he said do you think there's life on Mars? I said, well, there's a couple of wasps round the wrapper.

169. Church singers. They're an a-choired taste.

170. Last night I had a dream someone was saying, 'on your marks, get set, go'.
I woke up with a start.

171. I met a grumpy American. He was a Missouri guts.

172. So I saw this sad man in a refuse tip. He was down in the dumps.

173. I met a leech who was buying a Valentine's card. He was a sucker for romance.

174. This bloke said to me, he said I'm going to be a chimney sweep. I said, soot yourself.

175. I saw a bulrush in a library. I thought, that looks like a good reed.

176. My favourite band is called the Cockles and Mussels. I saw them alive alive-O in concert.

177. So I rang up the Fire Brigade. I said, my pet sparrow is stuck up a tree. He said, sparrows are supposed to live in trees. I said not Ian.

178. So I took up arable farming but I came a cropper.

179. This bloke kept hitting me with poultry. I got goose bumps.

180. This bloke said to me, he said do you want me to scrape both your knees? He was a double-grazing salesman.

JIGSAW PEACE

181. So I said to this bloke, I said what do
     you do for a living? He said I'm a DJ.
     I said who does the trousers?

182. Colonic immigration. We've got to flush
     them out.

183. So I said to Picasso, I said can you
     explain the out-of-shape faces?
     He said I think I'm about to sneeze.

184. I went to the doctors. I said, I feel as
     though people can't see me clearly.
     He said maybe you're a bit feint.

185. I had dinner at Uri Geller's house and
     I got soup all down my front.

SPOT THE DIFFERENCE

186. This judge said to me, he said do you swear to tell the truth? I said, no, I do it when I lose my temper.

187. So I said to this bloke, I said my favourite colour is a bluey green. He said azure? I said I'm certain.

188. I saw this mallard eating a burger. It was McDonald duck.

189. My agent said to me, he said you've been booked to do a gig in Versailles. I said, well, that's the Versailles knew about it.

190. Whenever I have a fight with someone I take a photo of it and put it in an album. It's my scrapbook.

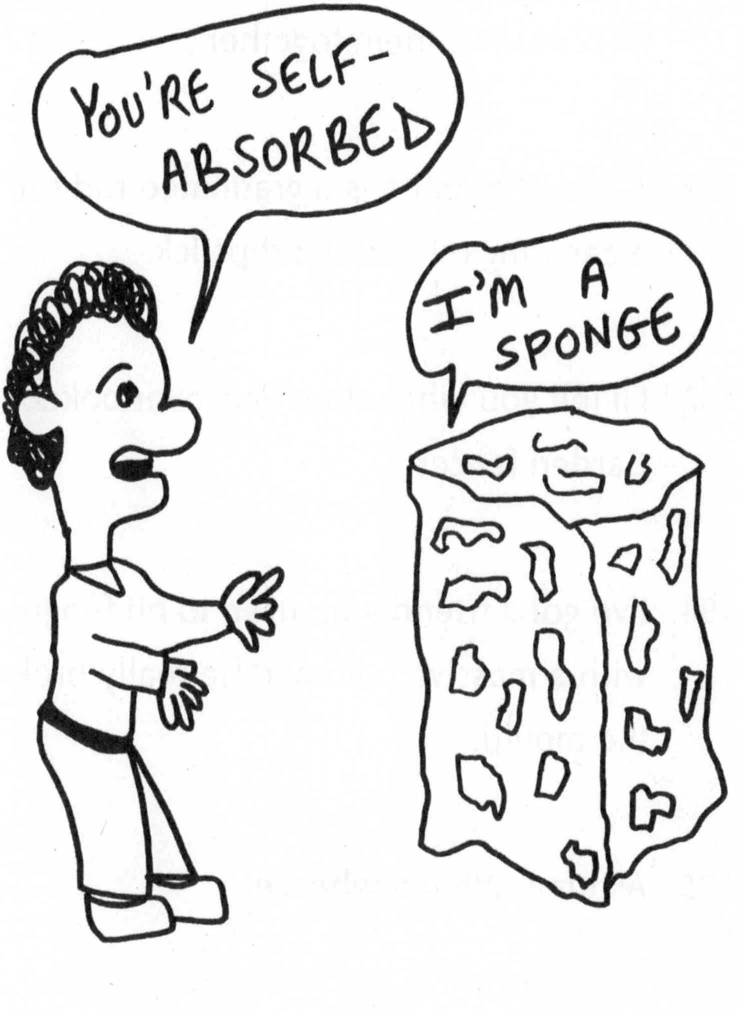
YOU'RE SELF-ABSORBED
I'M A SPONGE

191. I bought a double waterbed off Moses. Well, actually it was two singles but he'd pushed them together.

192. A friend of mine is a graduated rod for measuring oil. What a dipstick.

193. I'll tell you what often gets overlooked. Garden fences.

194. I've got a friend who used to hit fungus with a massive hammer. He really broke the mould.

195. Asthma. What a wheeze.

196. I know a woman who looks like a washing line. What's her name? Peggy.

197. I'm studying ceramics at the moment. It's driving me potty.

198. I went to a Hell's Angel's 40th. We sang 'Happy Birthday Tattoo You'.

199. Circus lions. They never get a fair crack of the whip.

200. So I was at home today leaning over the saucepan, stirring the food with my head. My dad walked in. He said, you'll never get married if you act like that. I said, I know. I'll always be a spatula.

AFTER DETOX.

TIM VINE JOKES: 201 TO 300

201. I went down the local fairground. I said, coconut shy? He said, put it like this, they don't go out much.

202. I said, have you got a Big Dipper? He said, don't be cheeky.

203. So I went to the Tarot card reader, I said it's my birthday today, can you tell me what the cards say? She said sure – 'To Tim, Happy Birthday, love from Granny.'

204. The rollercoaster was stuck upside down and all these people were hanging upside down with their hair standing on end. So I shouted up at them, 'You lot look really silly with your hair standing on end.' Then it came round again and they were all Mohicans and they beat me up.

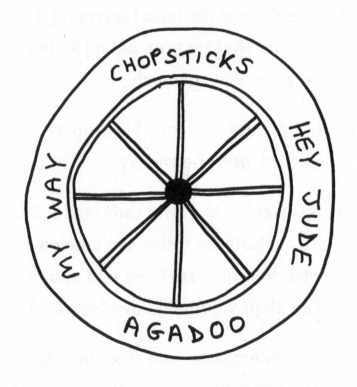

WHEEL OF 4 TUNES.

205. I had a go on one of those stalls where you shoot a duck over and you get a prize. I noticed if you aim the gun at the guy running the stall, you get ALL the prizes.

206. I left the fairground and I was beaten up by a local gang called the Hokey Cokey Gang and they all held hands and surrounded me. Then they put the left leg in and the left leg out, and they went in out, in out and they shook me all about. And every time I went, 'Ohhh', they went 'The Hokey Cokey'. And I thought, so that's what it's all about.

207. I've been living with a woman for some time. She's quite a bit older than me and we don't get on. It's my mum.

208. She said, I'm gonna dig a hole in the ground and fill it with water. I thought, she means well.

209. I said, I'm going to buy a theatre. She said, are you having me on? I said, I'll give you an audition but I can't promise.

210. The she fell on the floor so I rang up the hospital. I said, my mum's collapsed. He said, do you wanna stretcher? I said, that'll make her feel worse.

211. He said, what happened? I said, a row of books fell off the wall and landed on her head. He said, you've only got your shelf to blame.

CAT A LOG

212. I remember the first thing my mum said when I was born. She said, ah, I was expecting you.

213. When I left home, she said don't forget to write. I thought, it's a bit unlikely, it's a basic skill.

214. So I said to this bloke, I said I just got a job in a bowling alley. He said, ten pin? I said no, it's a permanent job.

215. My dad's liver is inside his left knee, his kidneys are on his elbows and his spleen is on the side of his head.
Still, his heart's in the right place.

216. My father is a soldier. He's not a real soldier. He's a thin strip of buttered toast.

217. The unluckiest person in my family is my uncle. Two weeks after he went blind, his guide dog went deaf.

218. I went to school with a bloke who had 2 arms, 2 legs but no head. It was very strange when he did cartwheels because you could never tell when he'd finished.

219. So this cowboy walked into a German car showroom. He said Audi.

220. I went to Alcoholics Anonymous. I said, I can't stop gambling. He said, you want Gamblers Anonymous. I said, you're probably right. I'm so drunk I don't know where I am.

221. So I went to the doctors. He said, you've got hypochondria. I said not that as well.

IRON MAN.

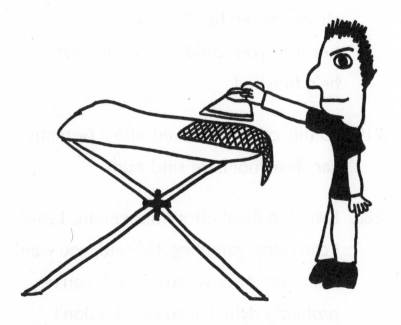

222. I said Doctor, I've just swallowed a Robin Reliant, what should I do? He said take it easy on corners.

223. I said Doctor, I feel like the whole world is ganging up on me. He said, hold on a minute ... Hey lads, he's in here.

224. I went blind recently and I had to go to a Braille opticians. I had to feel these huge Braille letters on the wall and they got smaller and smaller. When I got to the bottom I said, I can't read that line. He said, I'm sorry, I'm afraid you're gonna have to wear gloves.

225. Have you seen that new ventriloquist website? It's on Gubble-u, Gubble-u, Gubble-u, Got.

226. I don't do jokes about graphic designers – I draw the line at that.

227. I don't do jokes about Spain – No way, José.

228. I don't do jokes about an elephant who's packed his trunk and left the circus – Not on your Nellie.

229. And I don't do jokes about the verb to jump out and scare people – That's taboo.

230. I don't do jokes about a wooden step in the corner of the field that doesn't belong to me – That's not my style.

231. I went down the local music shop. I said, can you teach me how to read music? He said, why? I said, because I keep pronouncing it mussik.

20
KNOTS

Man leans into wind,
(before being hit by arrow.)

232. I said, I want to buy a violin. He said, do you want to buy a bow as well? I said, don't bother wrapping it.

233. I said, I want something that goes 'ping'. He said, ping? I said, you'll do.

234. I am actually a reverse vegetarian. I don't eat leather but when I go out I wear corned beef shoes.

235. When I woke up this morning I threw back my haddock skin duvet, put on my pilchard head slippers, splashed on a bit of cod liver oil aftershave and drew back the smoked kipper curtains and I thought to myself, life stinks.

236. This bloke said to me, he said what do you think of CFCs? I said, you're better off with O levels.

237. He said what do you think about
the problems with the Ozone?
I said, it doesn't affect me, I always
get a travelcard.

238. I got home and the phone was ringing.
I picked it up and said, who's speaking
please? And a voice said, you are.

239. So I rang up the local swimming baths.
I said, is that the local swimming
baths? He said, it depends where
you're calling from.

240. I said, have you got a diving board?
He said yes. I said, is it safe to use?
He said no. I said, why not? He said,
it's nowhere near the pool.

It's the fork that counts.

241. I said, how deep's your deep end?
He said, 6 foot. I said, how deep's your
shallow end? He said, 8 foot. I said,
how can you have a deep end that's 6
foot deep and a shallow end that's 8
foot deep? He said, the deep end's only
half full.

242. So I rang up my local building firm. I
said, I wanna skip outside my house.
He said, I'm not stopping you.

243. This bloke said to me, he said how
do you make quick-drying cement?
I said, there's no hard and fast rules.

244. I've got a baby cat called Kaboodle. The
other day I had to hold kitten Kaboodle.

245. I went out with a girl who lived on the
top of a tower block. She was high
maintenance.

246. I used to go out with a bouncy ball. She was all over the place.

247. I was going to run tours across my local Aztec cemetery. But I don't want to go over old ground.

248. This bloke said to me, he said I'm a herald angel. I thought, ooo, hark at him.

249. This cravat walked up to me and he was crying his eyes out. I can't stand emotional ties.

250. One bruise plus two bruises equals three bruises. It's a lump sum.

COMA TOES

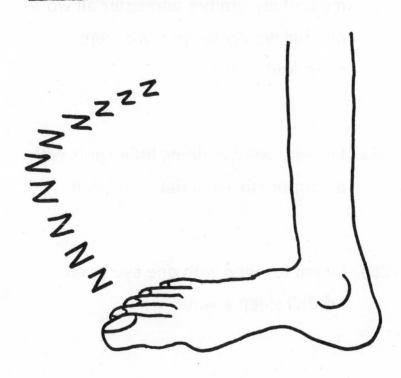

251. One Pope plus two Popes equals three Popes. That's Catholic maths.

252. When I was young my mum, my dad, me and my brother and sister all wore one big woolly jumper. We were a close-knit family.

253. I'm very good at doing little spots with a paintbrush. I'm a dab hand at it.

254. I went to sleep with one eye open. I didn't sleep a wink.

255. I thought Reuters were novelists from Birmingham.

256. I saw the musical 'Sweeney Todd' the other day. It was a bit hard to follow but I reckon the barber did it.

257. I'm scared of cattle. I'm a coward.

258. People who deal with dead bodies in hospital are always jolly. It's true what they say – The morgue the merrier.

259. My donkey loves Russian politics. His favourite is Trotsky.

260. So I was in Philadelphia. I said, can I stroke the Liberty Bell? He said feel free.

261. So I went down the local record shop.
I said, have you still got the Troggs?
He said how dare you.

262. I know exactly when my friends
are going to be sick. I'm a forensic
expert.

263. Conjuring. That should do the trick.

264. I don't swear, I promise.

265. So I went on a 10-week motivational
course. Well, I went to the first couple
of weeks.

SUN-GLASSES

266. I always say it's a marathon, not a sprint. That's why I lost my job as Usain Bolt's trainer.

267. Michael Jackson's Neverland. It was just a rich man's playground.

268. I've got a friend who's part of the gutter press. He's the editor of Drainpipe Weekly.

269. I'm a paranoid dyslexic. I have a feeling everyone is out to met gee.

270. My stage name used to be Nick Root. Everyone was late for my gigs because on the posters it said, 'SEE NICK ROOT'.

271. Macdonalds was broken into twice today. It was a double cheese burglary.

272. Where do pigs do their Christmas shopping? Hamleys.

273. The Incredible Hulk's masseur. He always gets the rub of the green.

274. This bloke said to me, he said do you want to buy a barometer? I said I think I'll take a rain check.

275. When I was young my mum didn't let me play with guns. I had to play with toy ones.

THE BOND GIRL OLYMPICS

The Gold medallist doing a lap of Honor Blackman.

276. This bloke said to me, he said have you seen that TV series called 'Exploding Shrapnel'? I said I've caught bits of it.

277. So I said to Tarzan, I said why are you painting a picture of your pants on a tree? He said you've got to draw the loin somewhere.

278. I can't remember my homing pigeon's name but I'm sure it'll come back to me.

279. Apparently Jupiter is the next big thing.

280. Legs up if you're double-jointed.

•

Which of these two blueberries
is the hardest to find?

281. Did you know Peter Pan had a brother called Deep?

282. I saw a pig in a demolition derby. What a crashing boar.

283. So I saw this bongo drum holding a pair of binoculars. He was a peeping tom-tom.

284. I've got a Christian mobile. It's pray as you go.

285. Nokia, and the door will be opened.

286. So I said to this anteater, I said how do you eat flying ants? And he just turned his nose up.

287. So I was in a Tube station and this bloke came up to me. He said, I've just been making some bread and now I need the toilet. I said you want the Bakerloo.

288. So I went down the local carpet shop. I said do you sell carpets by the yard? He said no, we sell them in here.

289. So I said to Vincent Van Gogh, I said does having one ear affect you? He said, can you say that again? I was only half-listening.

290. I went ice-skating today. I stepped on a banana skin and I stopped dead.

291. I went to a Swedish pantomime. It was called 'Snow White and the Sven Dwarves'.

292. I went down the local health spa and there was a sign outside which said 'Come in and be pampered'. I walked in and they attacked me with disposable nappies.

293. I just had a pudding in the desert. It was crème camel.

294. Ladies and gentlemen, please welcome house band The Conkers. They've had a string of hits.

295. I got an encore the other day. Well, I didn't actually get an encore. I walked off after two minutes and the promoter said, you'll have to do more than that.

296. So I went to the doctors. I said, I keep thinking I'm a German vodka. He said schnapps out of it.

297. This bloke said to me, he said what do you think of semaphore? I said I prefer Malaysia.

298. So I went to the local karaoke bar. I said, have you got 'More Than Words'? He said yes we also have music.

299. So I said to this barn owl, I said I've just got engaged. He said, you twit to who?

300. I said, it's this girl called Ena. Every time I see her I say, Hi Ena, and she laughs her head off.

TIM VINE JOKES: 301 TO 400

301. I went to a country in the Middle East and everyone was very boisterous. It was Rowdy Arabia.

302. I saw this sign. It said, 'Hairdressing for Men'. I walked in and there was a rabbit trying on clothes and all these blokes saying, yeah, very nice.

303. Last night I put everything I owned on one horse and it squashed it.

304. So I went down the local casino. I said, my girlfriend has just fallen asleep in the middle of a game of cards. He said poker? I said good idea.

305. He said, do you fancy a game of solitaire? I said, alright then, and he walked off.

THE 80'S REVIVAL

306. This policeman came up to me and gave me a thin piece of paper and a pencil. I said, what's that for? He said, I want you to help me trace someone.

307. A really handsome bloke sprinted past and I thought, he's dashing.

308. There was this bloke lying on the ground snogging a shrimp. I said, what are you doing? He said I've pulled a mussel.

309. So I was standing on my window ledge, six floors up, looking down at the traffic. I thought, one slip now and it's curtains for me. And if I fall the other way, I'm gonna die.

310. I went to the butchers. He said, I bet you 10 pounds you can't reach those 2 bits of meat. I said, I'm not betting. He said, why not? I said the steaks are too high.

311. Apparently 1 in 5 people in the world are Chinese, and there's 5 people in my family so it must be one of them. It's either my mum or my dad or my older brother Colin or my younger brother Hochachu. I think it's Colin.

312. I always get very emotional when I go to weddings. The last wedding I went to I cried my eyes out. It was when the vicar said, I'm afraid she hasn't turned up, Tim.

313. So I went to the cinema and I saw a very sad film. The bloke behind me suddenly started wailing. I got hit on the back of the head with a harpoon.

314. My girlfriend got in the car and her tights ripped, so I gave her the fan belt.

315. This bloke said to me, he said what do you think of 'Hello!' magazine? I said, it's okay.

316. So I was in my car and my boss rang up. He said, you've been promoted, and I swerved. Then he rang up a second time and he said, you've been promoted again, and I swerved again. Then he rang a third time and he said, you're Managing Director, and I went into a tree. The policeman came along and he said, what happened to you? I said, I careered off the road.

317. He said, I'm going to cut off one of your trouser legs and put it in a library. I said, that's a turn up for the books.

318. The back of his anorak was leaping up and down and people were chucking money to him. I said, do you earn a living doing that? He said yes, this is my lively hood.

319. So I was getting into my car and this bloke said to me, he said can you give me a lift? I said, sure, you look great, the world's your oyster, go for it.

320. Someone actually complimented me on my driving today. They left a little note on the windscreen. It said 'Parking Fine'. That was nice.

321. So I went down the local ice cream shop. I said, I want to buy an ice cream. He said, hundreds and thousands? I said, we'll start with one.

322. He said knicker bocker glory? I said, you do get a certain amount of freedom in these trousers, yes.

323. He said Tutti Frutti? I said, not so bad yourself Tiger.

324. He said Banana Dreamboat? I said, alright, pack it in.

325. So I went to the dentist. He said, say 'ah'. I said, why? He said, my dog's died.

326. Most dentist's chairs go up and down, don't they? The one I was in was going backwards and forwards. I thought, this is unusual and the dentist said, Mr Vine, get out the filing cabinet.

327. I was playing football on this aeroplane. It was amazing, I was running up the wing.

328. I'm on a special diet. I only eat things with the word 'special' in it. Special K, Special fried rice and of course, Marks & Spencer's Strawberry cream sponge cake – Special offer.

329. I said to my German friend, I said why have you got a piece of meat in the boot of your car? He said, that is my spare veal.

330. I've got a German Auntie, Auntie Aircraft Gun.

331. She gives me a lot of flak, that woman.

Look I'm doodling
my best alright!

332. So I was in Gibraltar and I said give me a whiskey. He said, on the rocks? I said, no, I'll have it here.

333. He said, do you like it neat? I said, yes. He said tuck your shirt in.

334. He gave me a pint of gravel. I said, what's that? He said one for the road.

335. So I was walking down the street and this woman stopped me. She said, excuse me, have you just washed your face with Imperial Leather soap? I said, yeah, can you smell it? She said, no, you've got the little label on your forehead.

336. You can't get Dairylea Triangles in Bermuda.

337. I bought some Bermuda shorts and when I took them off my pants had vanished.

338. Talking of drugs, if you take too much LDS you get dyslexia.

339. A lot's gone wrong for me today. The first thing that went wrong was my girlfriend got run over by a bus. The second thing that went wrong was I lost my job ... at the bus company.

340. Did you know, you can't get a job as an airline pilot if your name is Jack? Because you walk into the cockpit and the co-pilot says, 'Hi Jack', and everyone starts screaming.

341. You also can't get a job as an airline pilot if your name is Ivor Handgrenade.

2 CAMELS, A SHOWGIRL
AND A MAN DRESSED
AS A BEETROOT, HIDE
BEHIND A WALL.

342. I spent the whole of today at the filming of a Sugar Puffs advert. It's always fascinated me who the actor is who plays Honey Monster. So during filming I ran forward, got Honey Monster in a headlock, ripped his mask off, and it was Bungle from Rainbow.

343. So I went down the local garden centre. I said, I want to buy a garden. She said, we don't sell gardens. We sell things that are in gardens. I said, alright, I'll have a path.

344. I rang up the local ramblers club and this bloke went on and on.

345. You know when you're in love you get that tingly feeling all over your body. Well that's lead to me having 2 disastrous relationships with an electric fence and a cattle prod.

346. I remember once we had a candlelit dinner, so everything was undercooked.

347. My dog's not very intelligent, he only understands two words – Sit and Profitability. It took me ages to teach him to sit. For a long time he was running a small business standing up.

348. And he always misinterprets things that I say to him. I say, 'Heel' and he goes down the local hospital and does what he can.

349. I got home and he was sitting on the sofa. I said, get down! And he started dancing.

350. When I meet someone called Angela I get a temperature. I think I've got Girl Angela Fever.

351. I was adopted by my biological parents. My adoptive parents left when I was 12.

352. Dr Hook. What a guitarist. Mind you, he got through a lot of strings.

353. When I was at school, lessons were compulsory. You had to be there.

354. Did you know Demi Moore used to have a sister called Not Any?

355. I got up this morning and glued my letters together. I did a bit of mail bonding.

356. You should've been at the manicure world championships. What a nail-biting finish.

357. I did a gig on a boat and at the end they started shouting, More! More! I thought I was getting an encore and then I realised we were drifting away from the bank.

358. I bought an exercise DVD. On the cover it said 'Running Time 75 Minutes'. I thought, I can't run for that long.

359. History. History. History. Yes, history repeats itself.

360. Tiddles stole my manure and I'm speechless. The cat's got my dung.

361. This bloke said to me, he said who is your favourite African Star Wars character? I said it's Nairobi Wan Kenobi.

362. I won the Lottery, bought a wind tunnel and blew the lot.

363. The traffic on the way here was so slow we were overtaken by someone going in the opposite direction.

364. This bloke said to me, he said have you ever kept a diary? I said, no, at the end of the year I always throw them away.

365. A shepherd cooked me a pie. It was blackberry and apple. That was nice of him.

366. So Jarvis Cocker went to the doctor. He said, whenever I listen to my greatest hits my heart speeds up. The doctor said, those are Pulpitations.

367. Isn't it annoying when you're trying to kill a fly and he thinks you're applauding him?

368. The other day I was playing the violin. 'The Violin' is the name of a tune I can play on the penny whistle.

369. Osmosis. Is that when the Osmonds spread out?

370. Apparently when the Osmonds get an encore the audience shouts Mormon! Mormon!

371. I went to an Osmonds concert and the bloke next to me started shouting 'Crazy Horses'. I said shut up, I like them.

372. I tore my girlfriend's lingerie and I was done for criminal negligee.

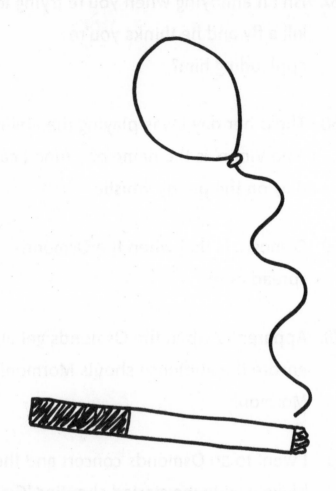

A balloon hovers above
an unlit cigarette.

373. Strolling in municipal gardens. It's a walk in the park.

374. Cold underground tombs. That's a bit cryptic.

375. Windblown heaths. They're very moorish.

376. Did you know the bestselling DVD this year is 'Poltergeist'? It's flying off the shelves.

377. I saw this cannibal biting his nails. I said, what's eating you? He said I am.

378. I remember when I played Noah in the school play. Ah, the memories are flooding back.

379. If you want to know how many bees Noah had – check the Ark hives.

380. At the moment I'm writing the stage version of the tornado film 'Twister'. I've got as far as the first draft.

381. There's a bit of a problem with the scenery but I'm sure it'll all blow over.

382. This bloke told me that I smelt like washing powder. It was so bio-degrading.

383. What do you call a 13 year old with his head chopped off? A guilloteenager. (That joke was well executed.)

384. I never tell people what I get up to at the top of small hills. What goes on tor stays on tor.

385. I saw a sign which said 'Professional Curtain Cleaning'. You don't really need the word 'Professional'. I'm sure no one cleans curtains for a laugh.

386. Every morning I rub a wild bird under my arms. Osprey-on deodorant.

387. People often ask me who's my favourite antelope band. It's Gazelles Aloud.

388. My girlfriend is half-woman, half-fish. I tell you what, it's mermaid all the difference.

389. There's something about an electric fence that I love but I can't put my finger on it.

THE DANGER OF DITTO

2	2
3	4
4	4
4	4
5	3
4	11
3	4
2	2

IT LOOKS LIKE ELEVEN.

390. When I was 40 I wanted to be an Egyptian. It was a pyramid-life crisis.

391. I saw a Greek comedian. He had a great sense of houmous.

392. It was non-stop taramasa-laughter.

393. This bloke came up to me and he said, meeoww! I thought, ooh, he's a bit catty.

394. Ever since I started working in an ejector-seat factory, sales have gone through the roof.

395. What's a Zulu's favourite chewing-gum flavour? Spearmint.

396. I'm always dropping cough sweets. I can't hold a Tune. (Tunes were 1970s throat lozenges.)

397. I tried to surf the Internet and I fell off my chair.

398. A lot of my fans are young horses. I've got a colt following.

399. This bloke said to me, he said if you ever get your own TV show can I appear on it? I said be my guest.

400. So I went to the mirror shop. I said, I want to buy a mirror you blonde lanky idiot. He said, I'm over here, sir.

TIM VINE JOKES: 401 TO 500

401. So I was reading the obituary column. It said, 'Mars bar, packet of Rolos, Double Decker'. Then I realised in fact I was reading the 'a bit chewy column'.

402. It said a lorry load of tortoises crashed into a train load of terrapins. I thought that's a turtle disaster.

403. So I was on the aeroplane and I was sitting next to this bloke who looked exactly like me. I said what's your name? He said Tim Vine. I was beside myself.

404. So I went to the watch shop. I said, I wanna buy a watch. He said, analogue? I said, no, just the watch.

405. So I was taking the M4 out of London and this bloke said, put it back.

406. I passed this man playing 'Dancing Queen' on the didgeridoo. I thought, that's Aboriginal.

407. Believe it or not there are twice as many eyebrows in the world as there are people.

408. This Alka Seltzer pill came up to me. He said, I bet you can't make me laugh. So I threw a cup of water over him and he just dissolved.

409. A long time ago I said to my father, I said I want to be a comedian. He said, practise in the bath. So I did and now I am one. He gave the same advice to my brother, but unfortunately he wanted to be an electrician.

DEAN MARTIAN

410. So I went to the doctors. I said, I'm scared of lapels. He said you've got cholera.

411. I said, the older I get the more I spread gossip. He said that's rheumatism.

412. I said, last night I dreamt I was eating a large marshmallow. He said, don't tell me, when you woke up your pillow was gone. I said no, when I woke up one of my large marshmallows was missing.

413. So I walked out and I was surrounded by protractors on motorbikes. It was Hell's Angles.

414. So I said to this bloke, I said what do you do for a living? He said, I sell manure. I said I bet you're rolling in it.

415. So I opened the front door when my Dad was in the middle of fixing it and he flew off the handle.

416. I went to a therapy group to help me cope with loneliness and no one else turned up.

417. I had a birthday party. There were so few people there we had to play keep the parcel.

418. So I went to the barber's. He said, do you want a crew cut? I said, no there's only me.

419. I said, have you got any Brylcream? He said it's not that good.

420. I said, give me a pony tail. He said, once upon a time this pony went to the seaside ...

TENPIN STRIKE

421. Today I met the bloke who invented crosswords. I can't remember his name. It was P something, T something, something something.

422. I was playing tennis and this 30-foot bicycle went past. I thought that's a long Raleigh.

423. I was halfway up this mountain and this bloke started attacking me. I said, what are you doing? He said, I don't like your altitude.

424. Then all these cows started falling over and scraping their knees. I said, what's up with them? He said they're grazing.

425. This bloke said to me, he said are you in favour of arranged marriages? I said, Yes I am, because I went to a marriage that wasn't arranged and it was chaos.

SCRABBLED EGG.

426. I was in this car wash and I started foaming at the mouth. I thought, I'm not having this, so I cycled out again.

427. I went to a four-star hotel and all the rooms were full of petrol.

428. The receptionist said to me, she said have you got a reservation? I said, yes. I'm worried about the price.

429. I said, can you give me an early morning call? She said, cockadoodledo. I said, very good.

430. I went to the local petrol station and there was nothing coming out of the nozzle. I walked in and I said, have you got your pumps on? He said, no, I'm wearing flip-flops.

431. I said super unleaded? He said, it is good, isn't it?

432. I went down my local beach and there was a young boy swimming on his own so I threw him a pair of binoculars. He said, what are these for? I said you need supervision.

433. So I went down the local shop. I said, I'm looking for a sailor with one arm. He said, it's not me. I'm a wholesaler.

434. He said, what do you think of voluntary work? I said, I wouldn't do it if you paid me.

435. So I was on this boat and all these bits of lamb started floating past. I thought, cor, it's getting choppy.

436. Whenever I get into bed I always think of France because my bedsprings go, 'Dordogne'.

437. So I went down the local pub. I drank a bottle of wine and lost my iPhone. I got arrested for being drunk and disorganised.

438. The policeman said, get in the back of the van. So I got in and there was a freezer full of choc-ices and a machine called Mr Whippy. He said, not that van.

439. So I went to the doctors. I said, I've got a rash. He said, I'll be as quick as I can.

440. So I was reading this book called 'The History of Glue' and I couldn't put it down.

441. I was born and bred in a bakery and raised in an oven.

442. We even had a pantry. It was a tree covered in pants.

443. I met this teenage goat and he had a human chin which is quite fashionable for goats. I said, ah, I see you've grown a blokey.

444. So I went down to the local electrical shop. I said, I'd like someone to sell me a kettle. He said Kenwood? I said where is he?

445. So I went to the pet shop. I said, give me a goldfish. He said, aquarium? I said, I don't care what star sign he is.

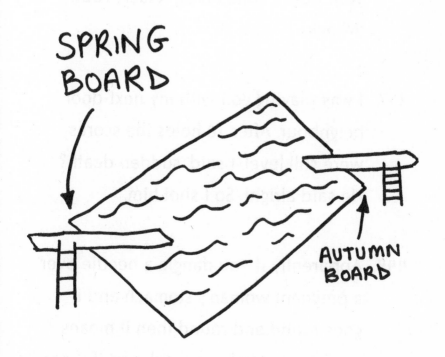

SPRING BOARD

AUTUMN BOARD

446. I said, I don't know whether to give my dog a tin of Pedigree Chum or give him a bone. He said, what's the name of your dog? I said, Knick, Knack, Paddy Whack.

447. I was playing golf with my next-door neighbour. After 18 holes the scores were still level. I said, sudden death? He said alright. So I shot him.

448. Apparently if you dangle a needle over a pregnant woman's stomach and it goes round and round then it means you're going to have a girl, and if it goes side to side it means you're going to have a boy. And if it gets pulled downwards it means she's going to have a magnet.

449. This midwife said to me, she said Tim, have you ever been present at the birth of a baby? I said, yes, once. She said, what was it like? I said, it was dark then suddenly very light.

450. I stuck all my photos in a book but found it really difficult to fill up another one. It's that tricky second album.

451. I won't be singing a freshly written little song tonight. This show contains no new ditty.

452. Why did Shaggy go to the underwater disco? He likes a Scuba do.

453. I went to India and I spent two hours haggling with a deaf street seller. A thousand pardons.

454. We've got a saying in my family. 'I want a divorce'.

455. I told my girlfriend to buy some Japanese food. Sushi did.

456. My grandpa had a bayonet. He caught eight bears with it.

457. Anger. It's all the rage.

458. So I went to the pet shop. I said, I want my money back for this budgie sunbed. He said that's a toasted sandwich maker.

459. I've got racist stockings. They're my Apartights.

CUP & SORCERER

460. They say life speeds up as you get older. Which is why you sometimes see a pensioner holding onto a lamp post.

461. Rolling hills. You wouldn't want to get in the way of one of them.

462. I was invited to a party. On the invite it said, 'Look Smart'. So I turned up in a lab coat holding a test tube.

463. You know when you put on a party invite, 'No Presents, Just Your Presence'. Well, I discovered it matters which way round you put those two words.

464. I cut a sheep's wool by accident. Shear fluke.

465. So I went to the bakers. I said, the loaf of bread I bought off you that's shaped like Winnie the Pooh has gone stale. He said, well, we've all got our crusty bear.

466. I went to a Middle Eastern shindig. It was a Lebanese-up.

467. I went to a Far Eastern shindig. It was a Cantonese-up.

468. I went to a shindig organised by Scrooge. It was an Ebeneze-up.

469. Have you seen that James Bond film about calculators? 'Casio Royale'.

470. So I said to my mum, I said I've bought you a tablecloth. She said that's a bit over the top.

HEADS WILL ROLL.

471. This bloke said to me, he said you're a stencil. I said cut it out.

472. I've always wanted to be a Hollywood waiter. So I've decided to get a job as a film star and hope a chef spots me.

473. When I run around naked I can be very cruel. I've got a ruthless streak.

474. This bloke said to me, he said I want to explore space. I said your mum must be over the moon.

475. Since I became a comedian the phone hasn't stopped ringing. It's broken.

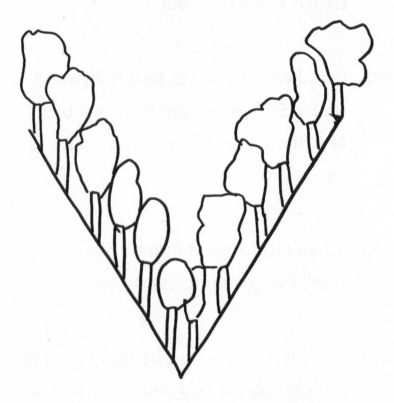

LOOKING UP A TREE-LINED
ROAD FROM THE
WRONG PERSPECTIVE.

476. This bloke said to me, he said your answer machine's recorded my voice! Your answer machine's recorded my voice! Your answer machine's recorded my voice! I said, alright, I've got the message.

477. So I said to this bloke, I said where are you from? He said, UK. I said, I'm fine thanks, how are you?

478. I saw a barrel of oil performing in a comedy club. He was slick but he was crude.

479. I'll tell you who's a cheesy performer. Mozzarella Fitzgerald.

480. So I bought a rocket salad and it took off vertically.

FUSSPOT

481. Welcome to 'OCD The Musical'. Starring, in order of height ...

482. This bloke said to me, he said I've drunk 90 gallons of soup. I said, you're full of it.

483. My dad's in charge of Sunday lunch. He rules the roast.

484. This bloke said to me, he said Tim, how often do you exaggerate? I said never ever ever.

485. So I said to Charles Darwin, I said what was before the Big Bang? He said God knows.

486. I saw a bloke kissing a mallard. I thought, love a duck.

RUGBY.

487. I used to drive a pizza delivery van. It was a delivery van made of pizza.

488. I was going to buy some slippers today but then I got cold feet.

489. Andrew Lloyd Webber's new musical is about a fizzy drink – 'The Fanta of the Opera'.

490. I went to school in a Wendy house. I found it hard to fit in.

491. The game Monopoly is all very well, but when are they going to bring out Stereopoly?

492. I keep getting deaf threats. Pardon?

493. If I ever find out what a Spoonerism is, I'll heat my cat.

494. Today I mended a violin, I restrung a violin and I polished a violin. Just fiddly jobs really.

495. Sometimes when I'm on the phone to a friend and a noisy motorbike drives past, I say, for a joke, wow, look at the size of that wasp. A friend of mine did that to me and then when I went round to his house, I discovered he'd been killed by a giant wasp.

496. There's a lot of trouble with guns and gangs nowadays. Even the Boy Scouts have a problem with it. That's why they sing that song, 'Gun gang gooly gooly gooly ...'

THE GARLIC PRESS.

497. Did you know if you set your mobile to 'vibrate' and drop it down a well, you'll never see it again.

498. Have you seen that film where sunburnt agricultural workers can change themselves into man-powered watercraft? 'Tanned Farmers. Rowboats In Disguise'.

499. If God had wanted us to re-use everything, he wouldn't have invented peaches.

500. Apparently stamps are worth more if they've been sent to someone. So I sent all my stamps to someone. And now he's got them.

501. My favourite party game is blind man's buff. That's when you find someone who's blind and then you polish them.

502. Do you ever go to McDonalds and when they say, do you want to eat it here or take it away? You say, I want to eat it here, and you eat your entire meal standing by the till.

503. So I went to the supermarket. I said, there's hair on this meat. He said let go of my leg.

504. I said, I wanna ring doughnut. He said there's a phone in the corner.

505. So I went to the off-licence and I said, Tenants? He said no, we own the place.

506. I used to live in a teapot. I know what you're thinking. Poor you.

507. I was christened with a flame-thrower. That was a baptism of fire.

508. And the vicar was wearing a gorilla suit, which was a blessing in disguise.

509. He was a Dutchman with inflatable shoes. One day he went for a run and popped his clogs.

510. So I ate this chess set and it was horrible. I took it back to the shop and I said, that's stale mate. He said, are you sure? I said check mate.

511. I said, I feel like an indecisive battery. He said, don't be so negative. I said, but I do. He said, are you sure? I said I'm positive.

512. My favourite composer is Handel who later teamed up with Hinge and Bracket to form the Doors.

513. I'm totally deaf, and I never thought I'd hear myself say that.

514. So I went to a fancy dress party dressed as sodium chloride. I walked in and this bloke threw sulphuric acid on my head. It was terrible. I didn't know how to react.

515. So I got home and discovered a burglar pressing one of my shirts. So I punched him, because you've got to strike while the iron's hot.

516. I saw this bloke chatting up a cheetah. I thought, he's trying to pull a fast one.

517. So I said to this train driver, I said I want to go to Paris. He said, Eurostar? I said, I've been on telly but I'm no Dean Martin.

518. At least the Eurostar's comfortable. It's murder on the Orient Express.

519. So I went down the local gym. I said, Mr Nasium ... can you teach me how to do the splits? He said, how flexible are you? I said I can't make Tuesdays.

520. I love climbing into a small suitcase. I can hardly contain myself.

521. I went to an Indian restaurant. I thought, this smells familiar. Do you ever get that? Déjà Vindaloo?

522. The waiter said to me, he said curry ok? I said, I might do 'Summer Lovin' when I've finished this.

523. You know those trick candles that you blow out and a couple of seconds later they come alight again. Well, the other day there was a fire at the factory that makes them.

524. My favourite film is the Clint Eastwood classic, 'Unforgiven'. At the moment they're working on a sequel. It's called 'Look, I Said I'm Sorry'.

525. So I met this gangster who pulls up the back of people's pants. It was Wedgie Kray.

526. So I went down the local video shop. I said, can I take out 'The Elephant Man'? He said, he's not your type.

527. I said, can I have 'Batman Forever'? He said no, you've got to bring it back tomorrow.

528. I said, what about 'Another 48 Hours'? He said tomorrow.

529. I said, have you got 'Big Trouble in Little China'? He said no, I'm just wearing tight trousers.

530. I said, 'The Hunt For Red October'? He said, I'll have a look in the stock room.

531. This bloke said to me, he said do you want a game of darts? I said, alright then, nearest to bull starts. I said, 'Baa', he said 'Mooo'. I said you're the closest.

532. I'm against hunting, in fact I'm a hunt saboteur. I go out the night before and shoot the fox.

533. The other day I sent my girlfriend a huge pile of snow and then I rang her up. I said, did you get my drift?

534. I went down the local supermarket. I said, I want to make a complaint. This vinegar's got lumps in it. He said, those are pickled onions.

535. So I bought some Armageddon cheese. On the packet it said 'best before end'.

A WAND CALLED FISHER

536. I got home and there was a dead chicken flying around the house. So I rang up the vicar. I said, get here quick I've got a poultrygeist.

537. So I went to the Chinese restaurant. I said, these noodles are a bit crunchy. He said, you're eating the chopsticks.

538. So I ordered and this duck walked up to me. He gave me a red rose and said, your eyes sparkle like diamonds. I said, waiter, I asked for aromatic duck.

539. I'm in a good mood today. I just entered a competition and won a year's supply of Marmite. One jar.

540. Did you know if a stick insect lays its eggs in a jar of Bovril, it will give birth to a litter of Twiglets.

DESIGN FOR WORLD'S
SCARIEST ROLLERCOASTER

541. This bloke said to me, he said can I come into your house and talk to you about your carpets? I thought, that's all I need, a Jehoovers Witness.

542. My next-door neighbour worships exhaust pipes. He's a Catholic converter.

543. So I rang up British Telecom. I said, I want to report a nuisance phone call. He said not you again.

544. I was having dinner with chess champion Gary Kasparov and we had a black and white check tablecloth. It took him 2 hours to pass me the salt.

545. He said, you remind me of a pepper pot. I said, I'll take that as condiment.

THE LIZARD OF OZ

546. So I said to this acrobat, I said have you got any winter pepper? He said no. I said somersault?

547. Did you know all male tennis players are witches. For example, Goran. Even he's a witch.

548. I've got a friend who's fallen in love with two school bags. He's bi-satchel.

549. So I was in Tescos and I saw this man and woman wrapped in a bar code. I said are you two an item?

550. In the morning my voice sounds like Barry White. Imagine what Barry White sounded like in the morning. Me, probably.

551. George Lucas has a snotty little brother. He's called George Mucus.

552. I remember being diagnosed with amnesia. That was a day to forget.

553. This bloke said to me, he said I'm going to start an agency that helps people who have marital problems. I said I can Relate to that.

554. I was in my car doing 30 miles an hour and a friend of mine phoned me. He said, I'm 5 miles ahead of you and I'm doing 29 miles an hour. I said I'll catch up with you later.

555. A huge pile of credit cards listing to one side. It's the leaning tower of VISA.

556. Herod went to the gym every morning. He was fit for a king.

557. The other day I had to fit as many schoolchildren into a classroom as I could. I hate filling in forms.

558. I watched 'Madame Butterfly' last night. In the first half she was a caterpillar.

559. My nephew is a man of very few words. He's six weeks old.

560. I went to a sweatshop and I bought two gallons of sweat.

CHERUBIC CUBE

561. This bloke said to me, he said I've changed myself into a pane of glass. I said, you've made yourself perfectly clear.

562. Time for the Bird of Prey Quiz. Fingers on buzzards ...

563. If you ever go for a walk with the Scissor Sisters, make sure they're pointing away from you.

564. Do you know the reason why Miss Piggy never got married? It's because she can't Kermit.

565. So this acorn said to me, he said whenever I'm underground I head away from the surface. I said grow up.

566. I tried yo-yo dieting, but it's not easy eating yo-yos. They tend to come back up again.

567. I saw this bloke laughing like a drain. He was going ... (make loud gurgling noise).

568. I haven't seen a cowboy film for ages. It's all quiet on the Western front.

569. I see the moving staircase debate is escalating.

570. I love it when people repeat what I've said but don't quote me on that.

LEMMING AT PSYCHIATRIST

571. If you ever split up with an anchor, let them down gently.

572. This bloke said to me, he said what's your favourite buzzword? I said Bzzzzzzz.

573. People are always using lingo and jargon. The trouble is, when Lin went she took the jar with her.

574. Every winter I adjust my car wheels so they don't slip on the ice. Snow chains there.

575. This bloke said to me, he said do you ever feel like you're 13 years old? I said a teeny bit.

576. So I said to this girl, I said I find the transparent part of your eyes that covers the iris very attractive. She said, cornea? I said, you must be an angel sent from Heaven.

577. They say if you're forced to play a musical instrument when you're at school, you're less likely to want to do it later in life. That's true of a lot of things. When I was at school I was forced to stick my head down the toilet.

578. I've just been on holiday across the pond. I spent two weeks in the tool shed.

579. I met this alien who couldn't stop swearing. He was an extra-Tourettestrial.

580. I find the hardest thing about voting with your feet is doing a handstand in the polling booth.

581. Sherlock Holmes keeps following me so I wrote him a letter. 'Dear Stalker ...'

582. There's too much wildlife in my garden. I can't get a bird in hedgeways.

583. I saw Sherlock Holmes crushing oranges. I said, what are you making? He said deduce.

584. I saw Watson on the street. I said, what's up? He said I've been Sherlocked out.

585. I went to the Amazon basin. Big taps.

586. I got stuck in a thick jungle. I couldn't hack it.

587. Sometimes I relax with a large curved knife. That's a scythe of relief.

588. (Sing) Knights in White, What Have I, Satin?

589. So I said to this air hostess, I said I can't see straight. She said, are you intoxicated? I said no I'm in economy.

590. Have you seen that television show where you run over an animal and then get it valued? Antiques Roadkill.

His school marks
were on the slide.

591. This bloke said to me, he said I'm fictional. I said get real.

592. Sometimes I lie at the top of a grassy bank and then rotate my body through several revolutions until I'm at the bottom. That's just the way I roll.

593. I went to the doctors. I said, people keep telling me to get down from things. He said come off it.

594. Apparently in Hawaii they like to honour Lulu.

595. In Russia there is a man on trial called Victor Aristov Christov Bannalutech Vich Volstoy Rievenskor. He's trying to clear his name. He'll need a big run-up.

596. I never eat oak, beech or sycamore. I'm treetotal.

597. I caught a cold on a carousel. I think there was something going round.

598. A dandelion. The king of the jungle wearing a cravat.

599. So I went down the local art gallery. I said, you've got a lovely view of the pond from here. He said, that's a painting. I said, well I'm glad you told me, because I was about to go outside and offer to help those chaps with their cart.

600. From now on I'm buying records, not CDs. And that's vinyl.

ANTI CLIMB AXE

601. I used to go out with an anaesthetist –
she was a local girl.

602. She was a knockout.

603. We had a lot of good times, in general.

604. If there are any more anaesthetic jokes,
I'm not conscious of them.

605. There are probably more somewhere
out there in the ether.

606. Anyone got any of their own in a
similar vein?

607. My local robin has opened a coffee shop in his house. Nestcafé.

608. I was walking down the street and I passed this man who was shouting, Marmite! 9 inches of it! I thought, that's laying it on a bit thick.

609. I've taken up speed reading. I can read 'War and Peace' in 20 seconds. It's only 3 words but it's a start.

610. I had a dream last night I was chopping up carrots with the Grim Reaper – dicing with death.

611. This bloke said to me, he said do you believe in ghosts? I said, of course I don't you silly Elizabethan sailor.

612. No man is an island. That's what my friend said to me and his name is Bob. Bob Ados.

613. When I was on holiday my girlfriend was hit by a tidal wave of tonic water. She got schwepped away.

614. I went to this church and this bloke threw hot ash on me. I was incensed.

615. Tiger Woods has got a terrible temper. I said to him, do you like golf buggies? And he went off on one.

616. I saw an advert which said 'Television For Sale, £1, but it's stuck on full volume.' How can you turn that down?

617. I'll tell you something that's worth its weight in gold – Gold.

618. You know those fake flames that you see in a restaurant? A piece of cloth blowing up through a light. Well, if you set fire to one of them it looks really unrealistic.

619. We're told in school that the coldest bit of the flame is the orange bit, which is a bit pointless cos it's still hot. I'm sure when Joan of Arc was burning at the stake no one shouted out, Joan, get in the orange bit!

620. When I was a teacher I had a nervous tic. Everyone got really good marks.

621. Everything has changed. Just look at the shops: Toys 'R' Us, Carpets 'R' Us and there's one near me that sells right angled triangles – Pythagoras.

622. Why did the cod have lovely skin?
Because he used human liver oil.

623. I bought my Latin-American manager a
Vauxhall – I got my boss a Nova.

624. I was gonna play my drums today but
somebody stole them. Bongos that
idea.

625. I've got a friend called Peter who
changes his name as often as he
changes his shirt. He's always been
called Peter, and he stinks.

626. I went to a pet shop and there was a
hamster in the window. It was literally
in the window. Double glazing, stuck
between the two panes.

627. I was playing tennis with a napkin and I said, hey, don't serviette!

628. Godzilla fell asleep on the M25 and he's left a huge tailback.

629. My mum and dad always do things straight away. I call them my immediate family.

630. So I was in this pub. I said, where's your bartender? He said, it's not tender anywhere, it hasn't got any feelings.

631. I was in Kenya and I spent two weeks on a Land Rover safari. What a waste of time, I didn't see any Land Rovers.

632. I bought a dog whistle. It's pointless. Whenever I put it in his mouth he just starts dribbling.

633. I used to run my car on lighter fuel. It works very well but on a windy day you've got to cup your hands round the bonnet.

634. I have got a friend called Lance but I don't see Lance a lot.

635. I've got a 7-foot fence round my garden and I could see my neighbour walking the other side of it. I said, are you 9 foot tall or on stilts? He said, both, I'm standing in a ditch.

636. I saw this guy in a suit of armour and he jumped over 30 double-decker buses. It was Medieval Knieval!

637. So I went to the bakers. I said, give me a sausage roll. He said, do you want me to put it in the microwave for you? I said, yes please, and he came home with me.

638. So I went to the music shop. I said, can I see your kettle drum? He said no, but would you like to see my toaster play the nose flute?

639. I was standing on the train station and the train came in so late that the driver had flowers in his hair and was singing 'Hey Jude'.

640. I went down the local swimming baths. I said, your chlorine is really getting up my nose. He said, she's got as much right to be there as you have.

641. I once had a job in a pet cemetery. Nothing much, I was a dogsbody.

642. Gene Vincent wrote Be-Bop-a-Lula while hanging upside down in the lion cage at Whipsnade Zoo. They don't write songs like that anymore.

643. I've got a friend who's very talkative when he goes up mountains. He's a social climber.

644. Rome wasn't built in a day. That's Milton Keynes you're thinking of.

645. I get my shoes specially made by a dentist and a carpenter. I have to fight tooth and nail for them.

646. A bit of advice. If a crocodile attacks you, jam a pencil in his mouth. Don't stick it behind his ear.

647. I did a gig in a zoo and I got babooned off.

648. I used to be a deep-sea diver but I couldn't stand the pressure.

649. I once played poker with my eyebrows.
I said I'll raise you.

650. Kenneth Williams was in a film about
someone making a chicken tikka.
It was a Curry On.

651. The reason they take organs from pigs
and give them to humans is because
pigs can't play organs.

652. My banjo said to me, he said Tim,
I'm leaving you. I said, why? He said,
because you're always picking on me.

653. I developed a picture of some cereal. It
was a bit grainy.

654. I think I may be a talented
photographer. I took just one photo
with my camera phone and it asked me
if I wanted to open a gallery.

655. So I went to the DVD shop. I said, can you recommend a Tom Cruise film? He said, 'Collateral'? I said what's the damage?

656. Last time I went to Macdonalds I destroyed the front of the shop and hospitalised four people. It's not my fault. There was a sign outside which said 'Drive In'.

657. I saw this man acting suspiciously next to Mount Everest. I said, what have you been up to? He said 8,000 feet.

658. I've got a friend who's very well-to-do. Or to be precise, he's got a lot of welding to do.

659. I've put something aside for a rainy day. It's an umbrella.

660. I've been out with a number of girls. One is the number.

661. I've been having trouble with hate mail. It's the price of stamps.

662. So I was sitting in the launderette watching the washing go round, and I thought, I should bring mine in here one day.

663. I've got lots of alternative friends. Or enemies as I call them.

664. Yesterday I cracked a joke. So I can't use it again.

665. Have you tried that new 007 glue? Bonds in seconds.

666. I'll tell you an actor who's rubbish. Dustbin Hoffman.

667. I saw a little tree with a guitar. Spruce Springsteen.

668. I went to a music shop and a man was putting blankets over all the electric guitars of a lower resonance. I said, what are you doing? He said, I'm just covering all basses.

669. You know when people say, step on the gas? How do you actually do that?

670. My favourite Beatles song is about lettuce, cucumber and tomato. It's called 'The Salad of John and Yoko'.

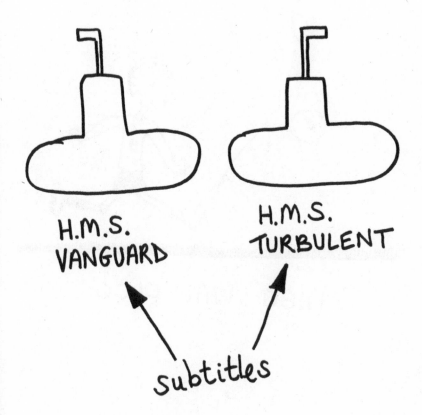

THEO WALLCLOCK

671. I've got a friend from Norway who only likes obscure Beatles songs. Well, a Norwegian would.

672. I saw Yoko Ono bathing her husband outside. I said, don't wash your dirty Lennon in public.

673. Maltese people. They don't melt in your hands.

674. The other day I proposed to an indigenous New Zealander.
I said will you Maori me?

675. I always wear a jacket to chase people. It's my pursuit.

676. (Exhale wistfully) Try that for sighs.

677. My girlfriend said to me, she said the trouble with you is you've got a glib answer to everything. I said it takes one to know one.

678. I tell my dog all my secrets. He's called Confido.

679. Yesterday I went round a roundabout 50 times. I was trying to win the Turner Prize.

680. I went to the doctors. I said, people keep asking me to join them in a steamroller. He said level with me ...

681. Release Richard Bacon – Hamnesty International.

682. Euromillions. It's a Lottery.

683. So I went down the local pub. I said, have you got a bar position available? He said, well no one's leaning on the jukebox at the moment.

684. This woman said to me, she said I'm a very tactile person. I thought ooh, touchy.

685. The person who works out my tax is an idiot by all accounts.

JACKSON FIVE

686. Your next breath of air. I'll just pause while you take that in.

687. There's a pirate I haven't seen for ages – Long Gone Silver.

688. The other day I got an invoice for a yak – Buffalo Bill.

689. Ugly. It's not looking good, is it?

690. One of the most dangerous games in the world is cyanide and seek.

691. The most dangerous winter sport is bobsleighing for apples.

692. So I saw this pond full of German cars. The water was murky.

693. If you're a witch, you've got to make sure you get your five daily potions.

694. Where does Robin Hood make his own curries? In Sharwood Forest.

695. I caught an infection at my karate class. It was kung flu.

696. I do portraits of boxers. I can knock them out really quickly.

697. Scientists have almost invented a supersonic male rabbit. In my opinion, they're just trying to make a quick buck.

698. So I went to the nightclub. I said, have you got a 70s night? He said, we used to. I said, when? He said in the 70s.

699. I've got a biro that doesn't write properly. It's a Bic pointless.

700. The trouble with an all-day breakfast is you've got to eat it so slowly.

701. So I went to the sweet shop, I said do you do Twix? He said, I'm quite good at juggling.

702. I went to Pizza Express and there was a sign outside. It said, 'Look Out For Our New Menu'. I walked in and it hit me on the back of the head.

703. I said, give me an American Hot. The next thing I know, big fat guy, Hawaiian shirt, 'Can somebody open a window?'

704. I ordered dessert and he gave me Tiramisu with a blindfolded horse. I said, no, mascarpone.

705. I went to an airport, I tripped over some luggage and I went flying.

THE SHEPHERDS HURDLED THE GOOD NEWS...

706. This taxi drove past and it was covered in chilli sauce. It was a mini kebab.

707. So I went to the doctors. I said, people keep talking to me about cereal crops. He said, migraine? I said don't you start.

708. When I look in the mirror I can't believe I used to weigh 28 stone ... because I didn't.

709. So I was reading a Bible in a hotel and I started feeling dizzy. It was a Gideon.

710. My vicar's disappeared. Somebody get me Missing Parsons.

711. The last thing my vicar said to me was, never eat probiotic yoghurt. Well, what he actually said to me was, never dabble in Yakult.

712. I normally play the trumpet with some buxom ladies. I am part of a big bras band.

713. I used to live with a rugby ball then I kicked her out. I said, stay in touch.

714. Rugby jokes – it's a nice try.

715. So I said to this bloke, I said how can I find out when's the next train from London to Glasgow? He said, why don't you look online? I said, that's a bit dangerous isn't it?

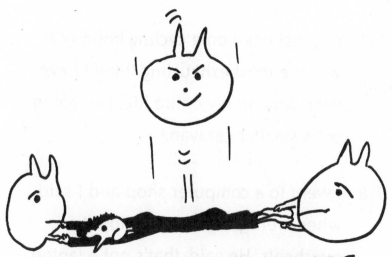

SPACEHOPPER'S REVENGE

716. A friend of mine always wanted to get run over by a steam train. When it happened he was chuffed to bits.

717. I've just been on a cycling holiday. It was the most exhausting thing I have ever done in my entire life. I've got to get a smaller caravan.

718. I went to a computer shop and I said, whenever I plug in my laptop it overheats. He said, that's not a laptop, it's a George Foreman Bar and Grill.

719. I said, where can I look up information? He said, Yahoo! I said, do you like that question?

720. This spaceship landed in front of me and out of it stepped a 20-foot cream bun. It was one of those extra cholesterols.

FIGUREHEAD

721. So this woman began to hover above me and she said, do you want to buy some moisturiser? I thought, she's having an out-of-Body-Shop experience.

722. I went down the local shop and I bought some blonde hair and blue eyes. I'm saving that for a special Caucasian.

723. I went to this shop that sells foreheads. He said, can I interest you in buying a forehead? I said no, I'm browsing.

724. If you want to confuse them in a charity shop, just hold up one of their old shoes and say, have you got this in a 10?

725. I once had a job as a driver for Spartacus. I know what you're thinking – Slave driver.

726. When I was in the Navy we were all named after our surnames. Harrison was Sailor 'H'. Williams was Sailor 'W'. And because I was Vine, I was Sailor 'V'.

727. The captain made me wear trousers that were far too small for me. He ran a tight ship.

728. He was actually a sheep and one day me and the other sailors threw him overboard. We were done for muttony.

729. I used to work in a garage which had a jet wash. It was pointless, there was nowhere for them to land.

3 weeks old.   2 weeks old.

THE ONE ON THE LEFT
IS THE ELDERBERRY.

730. People used to come in and ask me stupid questions. A bloke came in and said, what am I supposed to do with de-icer? I said put it on dee windscreen.

731. He said, what do you think of WD40? I said I quite like 'Red, Red Wine'.

732. I've got a job bursting people's boils for no charge – Freelance.

733. I'm on the 'Oliver Twist' diet. It's gruelling.

734. Do you know what's in a Waldorf salad? Walls and dwarfs.

735. So I saw this genie. He said, why am I so frightened? I said, it's obvious. Your bottle's gone.

Dear Doctor,
I just wanted to thank you for the pills that
you gave me to combat my tiredness. I'm
glad to report tha

736. You know when you're reading a book in the car it makes you feel sick. I find long before that happens, you crash.

737. I was standing at a bus stop and this bloke got a cigarette out and he looked at me and said, do you smoke yourself? I said what kind of lunatic smokes themselves?

738. So I went to a fancy dress party dressed as an oven. A friend of mine also came dressed as an oven, and he was really annoyed. He said, I thought you said you were coming as a parrot. I said no, what I said was 'I'm coming as a cooker too.'

739. Then these two sore lips walked passed. I said, hello chaps.

740. When it comes to cosmetic surgery a lot
of people turn their noses up.

741. Do you remember those days
when everyone had a tan?
The Bronze Age.

742. Bit of advice: never wear helium nail
polish at an auction.

743. I went to this party. It was full of
estate agents and belly dancers –
Movers and shakers.

744. I met a girl at a bungee-jumping club.
I said, are you attached? She said,
no I'm nooooottt. She was drop dead
gorgeous.

SOUNDBITE

The trampdening tower of Pisa.

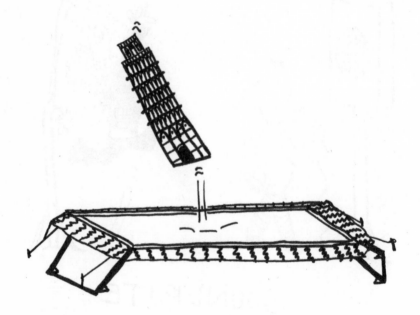

745. So I said to this estate agent, I said my house is in a terrible state. He said, what about a lick of paint? I said no thanks, have you got any toffees?

746. He said what colour is your living room? I said, off white. He said, how far off white? I said green.

747. In the end I sold the house for £100,000. I was very pleased with that because I was renting.

748. So I met a girl in a nightclub. I said, what's your name? She said, Chantelle. I said oh, go on.

749. I did further education. I went to Neptuniversity.

750. So I went to a fancy-dress party and everybody was dressed as a sore thumb except me. I stuck out like a vicar.

751. So I went to the pub and I said, can I have a pint of Pride? He said, it's finished but can I interest you in a glass of self-esteem?

752. I said, can I have a pint of 'Break for freedom'? He said it's run out.

753. Ladybird contracts. There's a lot of small print.

754. My dog got a job in a bank. The trouble is, he buried his bonus.

755. I've got a normal toilet. It's bog standard.

756. It's very easy to become addicted to helter-skelters. It's a downward spiral.

757. Last night I was eating a pancake and some bloke pushed me. Apparently it was Shove Tuesday.

758. So I went into my kitchen and I saw a hurricane making a pot of tea. I thought, hmm, there's a storm brewing.

759. The other day I did a lecture on colourful reefs. A few fish turned up to offer me some coral support.

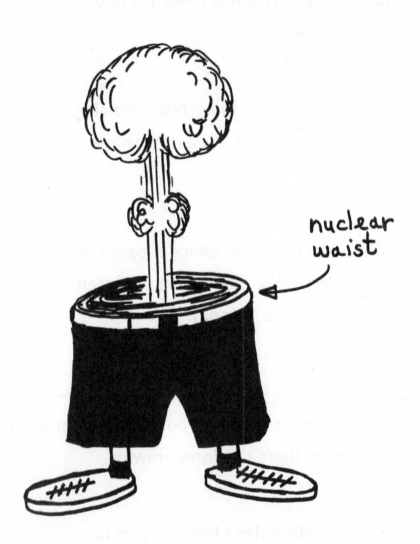

nuclear
waist

760. It's great to see so many familiar faces here tonight. The old two eyes, one nose and a mouth combo. It's still popular.

761. Last Sunday I went to church and it sounded beautiful because everyone was singing off the same hymn sheet.

762. So I said to this bloke, I said when I took my granny to Egypt she got very confused. He said, senile? I said yes, but she thought it was the Thames.

763. What do you call a deaf country singer? Dolly Pardon.

764. People used to call me names at school. They used to say, Oi! Names! Get over here.

765. The other day I saw a film about a dwarf on a zebra crossing. I wasn't that impressed. To me it was just a little pedestrian.

766. So I said to this bat, how's it hanging?

767. A friend said to me, he said I've just removed my son's ears and glued them to his chin. I said you're spoiling that child.

768. I was on a bus late last night. It was just me and the driver. It was really scary because he was sitting at the back with me.

769. This jellyfish walked into a shop. I thought, he's a slippery customer.

770. So I was weeping over this sergeant-major. Well, it's good to have a soldier to cry on.

771. My English teacher brought his dog into lessons. It was the teacher's pet.

772. I met an annoying peach. He was a pain in the nectarine.

773. I fell over in a bookies. It was a betting slip.

774. So I went to the camera shop. I said, shutter speed? He said we close at 5.

775. So I said to this bloke, I said I need a taxi. He said, flag one down. I said where am I going to get a flag?

CANARY FAIRY

776. I actually went to university three times in different disguises. When they found out they gave me the third degree.

777. You can say nosey and you can say eerie. But you can't say eye-ee.

778. They have a fire extinguisher at my church. They also have a brimstone extinguisher.

779. So I said to this castle, I said how come you haven't got any water round you? He said I've been de-moated.

780. I get seasick. And that's only after a couple of glasses.

781. A friend of mine has a very unsuccessful perfume shop. He's got more scents than money.

BELLY FLOP WORLD CHAMPIONSHIP

782. So I said to my girlfriend, I said why have you got chocolate on your chest? She said I'm wearing a Mars bra.

783. This bloke said to me, he said I'm never going to use a pen again. I said can I have that in writing?

784. So I said to this train, I said why are you late? He said sorry, I got sidetracked.

785. Mr Pecan, Mr Pistachio, Mr Cashew. What are you, nuts!

786. Be careful of the most important buffalo. He's a main yak.

787. I learnt the piano to grade 8. And that's quite a slope.

788. Why do porters get their own loos?

789. I bought a flat-screen aquarium. There wasn't enough room for the fish to turn round so they all ended up one end.

790. (Tim with boat on his head) Do you like my boater?

791. This chocolate went past at 100 miles an hour. It was a Ferrari Rocher.

792. A friend of mine and his wife got caught in the housing trap. I feel a bit guilty setting it but I wasn't expecting visitors.

793. My girlfriend has big ears, she's made of silver and she stands on a plinth. She's my trophy girlfriend.

794. Fields. They're as old as the hills.

795. I saw this bloke in a restaurant eating a television. He was having a set lunch.

796. This bloke said to me, he said I read in the paper that you overpumped a tyre. I said that's been blown out of all proportion.

797. I've invented a new flame-thrower. Unfortunately it hasn't set the world on fire.

798. This bag of rubbish came up to me. He said I'm at your disposal.

799. So I went to the Sauna Olympics. It was a proud moment. I was Steam Captain.

MASTERPIECE OF CAKE

800. The Bayeux Tapestry was bought by a farmer and that's how it got its name. They said, where do you want it? He said Bayeux.

TIM VINE JOKES: 801 TO 900

801. Bob Dylan's real name is Bob Zimmerman. His school photo is in a Zimmerman frame.

802. This bloke left a huge lump of plasticine in my dressing room – I don't know what to make of it.

803. So I said to this Scotsman, did you have spots when you were a teenager? He said ach nee.

804. I saw this bloke and he was shouting out 'Lambs for sale. Were 10 pounds, now 5 pounds.' I thought, that's sheep at half the price.

805. One armed butlers – they can take it but they can't dish it out.

MADCAP

806. What do you call a lady with big teeth who has a sleep after lunch?
Siesta Rantzen.

807. How come Tarzan was always grumpy?
Because he had a chimp on his shoulder.

808. So I said to Alexander Fleming, the inventor of antibiotics, I said I'd like to meet you on Tuesday. He said, hold on, I'll penicillin you in.

809. An alphabet grenade – if that goes off it could spell disaster.

810. So I rang up Alexander Graham Bell, the inventor of the first ever telephone. He said, where the hell are you calling from?

811. Velcro. What a rip-off.

812. This bloke said to me, he said whatever you do don't mention deodorant. I said, Sure, Mum's the word.

813. A friend of mine found a gold coin in a lump of earth – Lucky sod.

814. So I was mucking about in a lesson and the teacher made me stand outside. I was petrified. It was a flying lesson.

815. The advantage of easy origami is twofold.

NEVERTHELESS

816. So I went to the doctors and I said,
     I think I picked up an infection when I
     went swimming. I've got a swelling
     under my shoulder. He said, you're still
     wearing one of your arm bands.

817. This bloke said to me, he said do you
     want to use my ice rink for 10p?
     I thought, what a cheap skate.

818. So I was in this horse race and when I
     got to the finishing line I was hit by an
     apple seed – Pipped at the post.

819. I'd like to tell you a little bit about my
     personality. I'm a very private and
     secretive person ... that's it really.

820. During the Second World War my
     grandfather couldn't stop scribbling.
     He got hit by the doodlebug.

821. When I was in Vietnam, this fortune teller came up to me and he was on fire. He was a Napalm reader.

822. I'll tell you something that will warm your heart – Electrically heated lungs.

823. It's my girlfriend's birthday today. I bought her a giant helium balloon. That didn't go down very well.

824. So this bloke said to me, he said as a young boy was your mother very strict with you? I said, let me make one thing absolutely clear, my mother was never a young boy.

825. Mind you, she used to beat me with a telephone. I was always on the receiving end.

826. So I rang up the amputee help line and I got cut off.

827. Have you seen that new film where a transvestite plays hide and seek in a zoo? 'Crouching Tiger Hidden Drag Queen'.

828. So I bought this DVD and in the extras it said 'Deleted Scenes'. When I had a look there was nothing there.

829. Last night I dreamt I was the author of 'Lord of the Rings'. I was Tolkien in my sleep.

830. Well, you've got to have a hobbit.

JAM-PACKED

831. So I said to this bloke, I said did you know Marie Osmond is about to appear in the world's worst film? He said, Warner Brothers? I said, I already have.

832. So I went to a record shop. I said, what have you got by the Doors? He said, a bucket of sand and a fire blanket.

833. I said, can you recommend some music for a kid's party? He said, Small Faces? I said, of course they have, they're kids.

834. I said, I want some music to play in the car. I'm driving from London to Newcastle. He said, Bjork? I said no, B'Durham.

835. What's all this fuss about the iPod?
It plays 5000 songs in a random order
over a one month period. Correct me if
I'm wrong but isn't that called the
radio?

836. Do you know what slugs call snails?
Gypsies.

837. Have you seen the new reality TV show
where religious insects go climbing?
It's called 'I'm a Celibate Flea Get Me
Mountain Gear'.

838. I went to this squirrel nightclub. There
were hundreds of squirrels there. I said
to the squirrel barman, I said can I have
a bag of nuts? He said, to be honest
with you I can't remember where I put
them.

BALONEY

ABOVE
KNEE

839. My mum and dad are complete opposites. You couldn't hope to meet two such totally different blokes.

840. My local police chief does a talk on heroin so you can't understand any of it.

841. A friend of mine was killed by his own mum and dad. I blame the parents.

842. I was mugged recently at Victoria Station and I burst into tears. A policeman came up to me and said, I am fining you 10 pounds. I said, for crying out loud. He said yes.

843. I said, I've got to go to court on a drink driving charge. He said, is it the Old Bailey? I said no, Harveys Bristol Cream.

844. Tequila, Schnapps, Sambucca! I'm calling the shots.

845. So I said to this bloke, I said punch me in the face, so he punched me in the face. As I was lying on the ground I thought, I asked for that.

846. At the moment I'm reading 'My Life' by Bill Clinton, which freaked me out because I didn't know he knew anything about my life.

847. This bloke said to me, he said I've got bubonic plague. I said, don't give me that.

848. He said, I don't like interpreters. I said, speak for yourself.

849. He said, can you tell me what you call someone who comes from Corsica? I said course I can.

850. A friend of mine has three legs. He's always one step ahead of me.

851. This bloke said to me, he said how come your breakfast cereal is bleating? I said it's the porridge goats.

852. I've got really painful fingers. But that's my fault for giving an Indian head massage to a hedgehog.

853. This Roman emperor said to me, he said what's the weather like? I said hail, Caesar.

854. Do you ever lick an envelope and think it tastes so good that you eat the whole thing?

855. My favourite overweight 70s band were the Obesity Rollers.

856. The scariest cartoon I've ever seen was Gaddafi Duck.

857. Ever since I gave up bread I've lost loaves of weight.

858. I got food poisoning off an Italian dessert. I've a good mind to tiramisu the company.

859. This bloke said to me, he said I feel obliged to carry your golf clubs.
I said you have GOT to be caddying.

860. I'll tell you a great pick-me-up.
A crane.

861. I met this homeless secret agent. The name's Bond, Vagabond.

862. Did you hear about the woman who poisoned her husband with anti-freeze? Who was she married to, Frosty the Snowman? She should've just knocked his head off with a spade.

863. A tortoise on a running machine. Imagine how slow you'd have to set it for him not to fly off the back.

864. I used to be a vegetarian. But seeing two lambs playing together in a field put me right off it.

865. I've got an Elvis address book. The trouble is after I'd written Graceland in it I couldn't think of any others.

866. I was once caught stealing a horse. It was a fair clop.

867. Apparently mobile phones give you cancer. Mind you, you've got to smoke about 20 a day.

868. I like to dress up as Ray Davies and sing 'Waterloo Sunset'. Bit kinky.

869. Male cribs. They should be boycotted.

870. Katmandu. Catwoman doesn't.

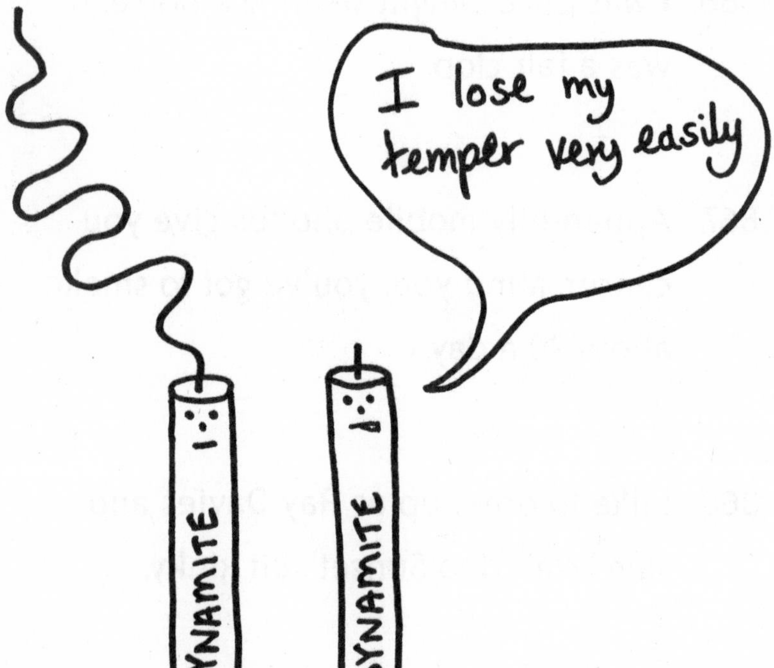
I lose my temper very easily
DYNAMITE
DYNAMITE

871. Pentecost. That's the spirit.

872. I tried to park at Cadbury's but it was choc-a-bloc.

873. So I said to this bloke, I said I'm going to open a chain of opticians across Europe. He said, franchise? I said, French eyes, English eyes, I don't care.

874. So Pi R Squared went round to a circle's house. He said, I was in the area ...

875. What do you call a little amphibian who never goes out? Hermit the Frog.

876. I was working in a shop and a bloke walked in and started punching everyone. I said, can I help you?
He said it's alright, I'm just bruising.

877. I once played cricket on the M25.
I was out for BMW.

878. Have you heard of that new style of cricket? The only way you can be out is by LBW, bowled or stumped. I know what you're thinking. Where's the catch?

879. Where does a dog go if his tail falls off? A retailer.

880. For a long time I thought Perth was where a woman with a lisp keeps her money.

881. There used to be a band called Half Man, Half Biscuit. But they broke up.

882. I think the greatest trick that David Copperfield ever did was getting Charles Dickens to write a book about him before he was born.

883. Ian Botham has got a brother. I don't just like Ian. I like Botham.

884. So I went to the insect barn dance. 'Take your partner by the thorax ...'

885. I'm actually taking anti-barn dance pills. I'm not allowed to exceed the stated dosey-dosage.

LINO TAMER

886. So I was in this folk club and the bloke next to me started humming. I said can you change your shirt?

887. I went to the Royal Albert Hall and it was full of pushchairs. It was Last Night of the Prams.

888. The Royal Albert Hall is massive, and that's just the hall. You should see the size of the Royal Albert Sitting Room.

889. I had a romance at the Highland Games. It was just a fling.

890. I saw a film called 'A Bridge Too Far'. The film before that, the whole cast drowned. It was called 'A Bridge Not Far Enough'.

891. My tortoise wrote a book. It was a hardback.

892. I'm allergic to aspirin. If I take it my head swells to five times its normal size. I take it all the time. My real head is the size of a walnut.

893. This bloke told me to look at the top of some mountains, so I had a peek.

894. I ran for Parliament once. I had to, I missed the bus.

895. So I said to Neil Armstrong, I said is it true the only man-made thing you could see from the Moon was the Great Wall of China? He said no. If I looked slightly to my left I could see a rocket and a moon buggy.

896. David Bowie writes songs by taking unconnected words out of a hat.
So 'Space Oddity' could have started, 'This is Ground Control to Flapjack Waterpistol.'

897. I've got an abacus made of Polos on a piece of string. I use it to work out menthol arithmetic.

898. I saw this cardboard cut-out in a baseball ground. It was the pitcher.

899. Elton John has a piano in every room of his house. He's even got one in the toilet, but when you leave you've got to remember to put the lid down.

900. I saw these bits of sheep around the top of a castle. It was the ramparts.

TIM VINE JOKES: 901 TO 1001

901. Did you know Leo Sayer has a brother called Sooth?

902. I went carol singing last year. I walked round lots of houses with a lantern and nobody gave me any money at all. Still, people are busy at Easter.

903. My mum takes things literally. The other day I said I'd like a cup of tea. She said, shall I make a pot? I said, yes please. And she was gone for half an hour trying to heat up the kiln.

904. The first colour TV transmission was not entirely successful. They were filming a zebra playing the piano on a giant chessboard.

905. My dog gives me a great massage.
'Up a bit, down a bit, stay!'

906. I once toured Austria with a theatre
company and the scenery was fantastic.
We used to keep it in a horse box.

907. So I went down the local bank.
I said, can I make a withdrawal?
He said yes. So I walked out again.

908. I see the US president is starring in
a new ABBA musical. It's called
'Obama Mia'.

909. I once sang in a close harmony singing
group. Very close. We used to practise
in a phone booth.

910. Cleopatra used to bathe in goats' milk. She once fell asleep in the Jacuzzi and woke up in a tub of margarine.

911. Radioactivity. Is that when your radio starts going out and doing stuff?

912. There's a new TV show where you have to dress up as Russian kings. It's called 'Tzars In Your Eyes'.

913. If wine is plonk, does that mean wine tasters are plonkers?

914. Did you know plutonium is extracted from the saliva of Disney dogs?

They were both showing signs of strain.

915. The Great Train Robbers stole
2.5 million pounds. In fact it was
more than that because they didn't
have any tickets.

916. So I went to the hospital and I had an
X-ray. The doctor went behind a screen
and I heard some buzzing. I said, is it
finished? He said no, I'm just having a
shave.

917. Sandals are called sandals because if
you don't wear them on the beach,
sand'll get in-between your toes.

918. I made a stew out of a team of rugby
players. It was scrummy.

919. Last time I had a street party I nearly
died. I live on the M20.

920. My sister lives in a pillar box. I don't see much of her.

921. I used to leapfrog over pillar boxes. Last time I did it I broke my nose and two of my ribs, because I tried to leapfrog one of those little square ones stuck to a wall.

922. My telephone tells me if the host of 'Big Brother' is trying to ring. It's got Davina McCall waiting.

923. The Beatles did an Australian tour. John, Paul, George and Dingo.

924. I did a gig in the Bastille. Stormed it.

PRAISE & WARSHIP

925. San Tropez has a topless beach.
There's no sand on it.

926. Frank Whittle invented the jet engine.
A few years later he invented the
hairdryer and blew his wife's
head off.

927. I went out with an MP from Blackpool.
She was a stick of rock. What a lovely
candy date.

928. Bear meat is lovely. Although it is a
bit grizzly.

929. You know when you're tossing a
pancake and it gets stuck to the ceiling?
That happened to me once. I got stuck
to the ceiling.

930. So I said to this bloke, I said I was running away from a volcano and I tripped on a rock. He said, Krakatoa? I said no but I twisted my ankle.

931. I asked Linford Christie to buy me some frozen peas and he took ages coming back. I said where's that runner been?

932. I used to want to be a robber in Mexico but they've bandit.

933. I once danced the tango on an underwater shipwreck. Shoal, shoal, squid squid shoal.

934. Nelson had five children but only one of them was called Horatio. That's Horatio of one to five.

HANDLEBAR
MOUSTACHE

PEDAL
EYEBROWS

935. So I said to this bloke, I said me and a friend just cycled across the desert with our legs exposed. He said, tandem? I said we certainly did.

936. So I went to the doctors. I said, I got hurt in a pillow fight. He said you've got concushion.

937. I saw this film about prehistoric pigs. 'Jurassic Pork'.

938. So I said to this bloke, I said I bet you'd like to see where Dick Turpin lived. He said, sure would. I said no, that's Robin Hood.

939. In today's tombola, first prize is an Indian headdress. So we'll be raffling some feathers tonight.

940. They're terribly behaved in the House of Lords. It's not their fault, it's peer pressure.

941. Dynamite was invented by Alfred Nobel. At first he didn't have a name for it. Then it blew his house up and he said, this stuff's dynamite.

942. I went to a drive-in movie. I didn't see much. There was a bloke in the front row in a combine harvester.

943. The last book I read was an encyclopaedia. I know what you're thinking. That explains everything.

944. If you've got a rabbit it's very bad to carry them around by their ears. It makes them lazy.

945. They say all the world's a stage. So how come we're not all facing the same way?

946. Champagne makes you dizzy but it's cheaper to run in circles.

947. Cher had two ribs removed to make her look thinner. She said, I'm not eating those, take them away.

948. People want to swim with dolphins because it's a unique experience. But it's not as unique as white-water rafting with a duck-billed platypus. I miss Genghis.

949. So I went to the pet shop and I said, how much is that doggy in the window? He said, the one with the waggly tail? I said no, the one next to it.

950. This bloke said to me, he said do you like fencing? I said sword of.

951. I tried playing the piano with a broken foot but I couldn't sustain it.

952. This bloke said to me, he said I'm mute. I thought, that goes without saying.

953. I can speak Swahelium. It's like Swahili but a bit higher.

954. Coffee. It's not my cup of tea.

955. This weatherman walked up to me holding a huge ridge of low pressure. He had some front.

956. Molecules, atoms, protons, neutrons –
I'm rubbish at small talk.

957. My favourite Russian song is 'Crimea
River'.

958. So I said to this bloke, I said a bird like
a swallow just flew past. He said, swift?
I said like the clappers.

959. I've got a friend and all he ever wants
to do is dress up as a small black
insect and live under a rock. He's just a
bit anti.

960. Censorship makes me so bleeping
angry.

BRITISH AEROSPACE

961. The school I went to was a picture made of coloured paper and seashells stuck on with glue. It was a sixth-form collage.

962. After I left university I removed one of my front teeth for 12 months. It was my gap year.

963. When I was born my mum lit a stick of dynamite and put it in my mouth. I was part of the baby BOOM!

964. I'm glad I wasn't a fly on the wall when they invented fly spray.

965. I went to a tug-of-war competition and I pulled.

966. Tweet, tweet, tweet. A little bird told me that.

967. So I woke up in the jungle and I was covered in bites. Those tigers.

968. This bloke said to me, he said I'm going to blindfold you, spin you round in circles and leave you in a field 50 miles away. I said you've lost me there.

969. So I was up all night wondering what happened to the sun and suddenly it dawned on me.

970. The other day I played golf with a female dog. It was bitch and putt.

971. Whenever I cry, little wooden huts drop out of my eyes. A lot of tears have been shed.

972. A friend of mine killed himself in the desert. He was a camelkazi.

973. So I went to the doctors, I said I've got a pain in my stomach and I think I'm a small wading bird. He said you've got a coot appendicitis.

974. I said I can hear music at the base of my spine. He said you've got a slipped disco.

975. I said, I always put an 's' on the end of words. He said you've pluralsy.

976. I hate it when people stand on things to make them look taller. I really think people shouldn't do that. Alright, I'll get off my soapbox now.

977. I've just eaten an abacus. I've always said it's what's inside that counts.

978. I've planted a redwood in Buckingham Palace garden and I was arrested for high treeson.

979. I've got a friend who's a pointless beam of light. Laser good-for-nothing.

980. I had a polio injection the other day and I can't even ride a horse.

981. I went to a nightclub during the day and there was no one there.

982. Why do you never see an elephant on a bus? Because he's got a massive bum.

983. I forced Mike Tyson to do bell ringing at my church. I said, I've got you on the ropes now, haven't I?

984. I went to bed with a grindstone. The next day I got out of bed sharpish.

985. Yesterday I fired my cleaner. I'm glad that's done and dusted.

986. I went to a party in a pendulum. When I got there it was already in full swing.

987. It's amazing how many poems have been written by a nun.
(Oh, it's anon is it?)

988. Infinity, forever, eternal, immortal.
The list is endless.

989. I'm terrible at line dancing. I keep going off the page.

990. My house has just been infested by an Italian sauce. So I rang up Pesto Control.

991. I've got an eating disorder. I go coffee first, then pudding, then main course.

992. I finally got on the property ladder.
I'm a window cleaner.

993. What goes around comes around.
Look at Swingball.

994. So I jumped over a bottle of whiskey on
one leg – Hopscotch.

995. Cliff Richard said if it wasn't for Elvis
Presley there would never have been
Cliff Richard. But I don't think you can
blame Elvis for that.

996. This bloke said to me, he said have you
ever had a nosebleed in an unusual
place? I said no, it's always my nose.

997. I got attacked by a lumberjack from Warsaw. I was Pole-axed.

998. The other day a tornado hit my local fair. It was a cruel twister fête.

999. Did you know Steve the Gingerbread Man has just been voted London's most edible bachelor?

1000. Someone threw Chinese soup at me. It was won-ton violence.

1001. I had a haircut at Christmas. All the trimmings.

ACKNOWLEDGEMENTS

Thanks for extra contributions go to John Archer, Karl Hampson, Sonya Vine, James Suart, Mark Kelly, Graham Noon, Michael Sell, Dawn Booth and Roy Grindrod.

To each, I award the gold star of pun-writing.

And thanks also to Tim Payne for this and everything else.

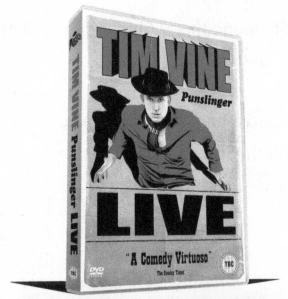